WILLIA...

Deep
Currents
of the
Spirit

©2024 William N. Rapien. All rights reserved.

Edited by Michelle Schacht.

Unless otherwise indicated, Scripture verses quoted are from the *King James Version* of the Bible.

All Hebrew and Greek definitions are from Strong's Exhaustive Concordance of the Bible with Greek and Hebrew Dictionaries, Royal Publishers, Inc. (January 1, 1975)

ISBN: 979-8-9904413-1-6 (paperback)
ISBN: 979-8-9904413-0-9 (hardcover)
ISBN: 979-8-9904413-2-3 (ebook)

CONTENTS

Acknowledgements

I would like to thank a couple of my friends who, over the years I have spent on this project, have proofread the chapters and provided support to me. First, I want to thank **Emily Gerry** from Umatilla, Florida who is a retired librarian and a sister in Christ. She gave me a lot of support and input from the very beginning seven years ago. We attended the Church at Whistling Pines in Umatilla together and were part of a life group there.

Let me also thank **Delia Santiago**, who provided a critical eye and assisted me with correlating the English and the initial Spanish translations. Delia worked with me many years ago in the Digital Equipment Corporation manufacturing plant in Aguadilla, Puerto Rico. She is fully bilingual in the English and Spanish languages and has over twenty (20) years working in the Administrative and Clerical field. I was blessed when, after many years, she and her husband knocked on my door. That was a wonderful surprise. It was good to see she was just as fervent in her faith as I remembered. She immediately took on the challenge of going through the book and adding valuable insight to my writing as well. Her encouragement helped me through a few challenging chapters.

I would also like to thank my editor **Michelle Schacht** who I found through Reedsy. I thought I had the book ready for publication but she found all kinds of issues with formatting, punctuation and grammar. It was so helpful to find someone who did not know me and could provide and unbiased viewpoint. The book is easier to read and to understand due to her efforts. She also helped me to understand the steps I needed to take to get the book ready for publication.

I want to thank **Rosemary Strohm** who designed the cover and did the layout for me. I am glad there is someone like her who is artistic.

Most of all, I want to thank the Holy Spirit for the inspiration and revelation I needed to actually begin this journey and to stay on the correct path to finish the book. Never in my wildest dreams had I thought I would write a book such as this one.

Introduction

I am perhaps not the most likely of people to write a book of this nature. I have no degree in theology or religion. I have never even written a book before. All I have is the experience of my walk with Christ. Over the years, I have learned the doctrines of the various denominations as a layman, moving from church to church, seeking to find that special knowledge I needed to show God's power in my life but never finding what I was seeking. I have been involved with founding a church and have served as an elder in a few churches. I found myself wishing I had been able to walk with Him as the disciples did and to be able to ask Him directly what He meant in His teachings.

Although I remained a faithful member of a congregation and tried to actively participate within the constraints of the doctrines and dogma of the church I attended, I came to understand there was something important missing. There was no power in my life like the believers in the early church had. There was no evidence of the reality of God in my walk. I was a user of drugs, could not quit smoking, and sinned constantly, and did not seem to have the power to stop myself. I yearned to be free of my sin but found myself constantly returning to do those things that religion told me I must stop doing. I was outwardly religious but I was not able to free myself from my sin.

One day, I finally reached the end of my strength in my struggle with sin. As I helplessly cried out to God for deliverance from myself, from this nature within me that I could not change, God responded. He had not seemed to hear my prayers for strength as I struggled to deliver myself from my sin. He had not seemed to see me in the positions I held or in the responsibilities I performed within the local church. But He saw me when I cried out in my despair, when I finally gave up trying to conquer my sin by my own strength. He began to deliver me from those addictions and heal my body. He even delivered me from being tempted by those things I could never seem to resist.

I realized then that what the modern-day Christian church was teaching was not correct. We cannot save ourselves. Our will is powerless unless it is fully submitted to God's will. The gospel is not about motivating us to be better people. The gospel is about the power of God coming into this world to deliver us from ourselves. We desperately need God to deliver us.

I began to search for God, not within the teachings of the modern-day church but within Scripture. I re-examined the Word, consciously putting aside the theology and the doctrine the church taught to see what the Word said on its own. I sought the aid of the Holy Spirit to reveal the truth of the Word and of God's purpose for me. Thus, my journey toward God began.

I sought the truth of God. I studied the Word, memorized the Word, and meditated on the Word. As time passed, I discovered I could hear God's voice speaking directly to me. I held daily conversations with Him and developed a relationship with Him that I thought was only reserved for the most holy of people. I remained a sinner but I was striving to enter into His presence, to know Him personally. And He did not reject me because of my sin, because of my sin nature. I found out that everyone, including me, could know God!

The modern-day church relies on intellectual dogma and worldly philosophies to present a watered-down message of salvation to their congregations. Its doctrine is based on the personal revelation of those who went before them (such as Luther) but without its members own personal revelations. At the same time, its doctrine declares all has been revealed in the Bible and that personal revelation is no longer needed. Only the church knows the truth and anyone who contradicts the church is anti-Christ. Of course, I speak of the church, of religion, in general.

It is not my intent to nail this book to the doors of religion as Luther did in his time. I only pray that, as I share what I learned in studying the Scripture, the Holy Spirit will lead you, the reader, to begin the same journey towards knowing God instead of settling for just knowing about God. So, put aside the tinted lenses of theology and join me in simply reading the Word from a new perspective. Seek to understand what is sin and why God had to send His Son to restore us to true communion with Him.

I invite you to join me in understanding the gospel according to Jesus, the Christ.

The Bad News

Perhaps the greatest problem in sharing the Good News is that the unbeliever is usually not aware of their fallen condition or of their need for God. The unbeliever only knows what they have learned from their family, friends, classmates, coworkers, and other elements of society surrounding them. Media and entertainment are the primary sources defining good and bad in the modern world. The world tells people to seek power, money, and sex and that they will be happy when they succeed in this. And yes, while they may have been exposed to religious teachings, they usually are only exposed to these ideas for a very small amount of time compared to the other sources.

When people begin to seek God, it is usually out of desperation for an answer to their problems or out of fear of the consequences of their actions. Often, the desire for peace and forgiveness leads them to one of a multitude of different religions but not to God. But the guilt does not go away and there is still the sense that the answer has eluded them.

This continues to be true even when they accept Jesus as their Lord and Savior in most churches because the Good News is watered down. Also, it is exceedingly rare for someone to accept the Good News of Christ based upon a logical argument or by coming to a philosophical conclusion as some religions attempt.

It is only with the help of the Holy Spirit, who reproves the world of its sin, that we can share the Good News with the unbeliever. The world's sin is defined in John 16:8 as not believing in the complete work of Jesus. In John 16:8, the word "reprove" in Greek is ἐλέγχω, which means to convict, convince, tell a fault, rebuke, or reprove. Many bible translations translate this word as "convict." This word is not meant to be understood as a criminal judgment but as having a conviction concerning something, in this case that Jesus truly opened the way to a restored relationship with God. Our task is to allow the Spirit to use us to bring the unbeliever into Christ's redemption and into a restored relationship with God. We need to be prepared to be used by the Holy Spirit in His task of reproving the world of its sin. To do this, we need to show men why the Good News is good news. We need to share the bad news first so they may understand why they need Jesus.

Believing in God or in a god or gods is not the same thing as knowing God. Whether you believe God exists or not isn't sufficient for salvation. It does not matter if you have never believed in God, or if you consider yourself a member of a religion, or even a member of a Christian denomination. It is not about knowing about God in an intellectual or theological way but about knowing Him as in having a daily personal relationship with Him. If you do not know God, you are separated from God.

The agnostic or atheist unbeliever only follows what the world system says is currently socially acceptable behavior. A culturally dependent definition of right and wrong is all that guides them. Although the cultural definition may be based on moral principles derived from religious texts, these unbelievers view those principles as inventions to control man and their social interactions. Those who practice behaviors which are currently socially unacceptable actively try to change the definition of what is right and wrong in order to justify or legitimize their own behaviors. Therefore, the world system is constantly changing its definition of what is acceptable behavior. The historical lessons of past civilizations that fell into decay due to social immorality and inconsistency are ignored in the pursuit of fulfilling their own will in modern context. The Bible is not viewed as anything other than a book written by man and the moral principles taught by the Word of God are considered old fashioned and irrelevant to today's society.

The desire to redefine what is right and wrong is not restricted solely to the agnostic or atheist unbeliever. Many believers have fallen to the temptations of the world system and have been instrumental in introducing this mindset into the church. The powers and principalities of this world have always attacked the church, but it is especially evident in these latter days. For example, sexual immorality is clearly defined in the Bible as an abomination to God and yet there are Christian denominations making every effort to be "all inclusive", even ordaining homosexuals. And this is not the only type of immoral behavior infiltrating today's society and today's churches. If believers do not have a real relationship with God, they are no better off than the unbeliever.

While the unbeliever does not believe in sin, the believer may accept they are sinners but most likely do not fully understand what sin is and, therefore, the full significance of the Good News. This group believes sin is defined by biblical law and they need to stop sinning by an effort of their own will. These believers' understanding of the nature of their sin and their redemption and restoration is superficial. They follow what other men teach and adhere to a denomination's doctrine, but they do not enter into the presence of God, preferring that their pastor or priest go to God to bring back something for them to hear. They do not want to dedicate time to search for God and develop a relationship with Him. They are satisfied with a religious experience and miss out on the incredible personal experience God desires to have with them.

This is compounded further for those who believe in God but who believe they have never sinned and therefore have no need to repent. These people have been raised in the church and are often very religious. The Bible clearly says in Romans 3:23 that all have sinned and fallen short of the glory of God, but they still believe they have avoided sin by obedience to biblical law through the strength of their own will. They do not believe they need to accept the redeeming work of Christ either because their parents already did that for them or because they believe they have avoided sin. They are the modern-day equivalent of the Pharisees and Sadducees.

Blessed is he who is convinced of his need for God and fully accepts the Good News. He acknowledges his sinful nature and comes to God through Christ with the hope of salvation. Although he will often not understand the true nature of sin and the true nature of his salvation, he accepts Christ's payment for his sin.

Frequently, believers are misled because those who should be teaching them the truth cannot because they themselves do not understand the truth. They believe and teach that the result of Adam's sin was man's eternal damnation in hell. This group is taught that Jesus saved them from hell, and, as long as they abide by the doctrines of the church they belong to, they are fine. As a result, they substitute an outward religious expression for the inward relational experience of walking with God. This is the sad state of affairs in the body of Christ today.

THE GOOD NEWS

To understand the Good News, we need to understand why it is good news. To do that, we need to understand what the bad news is that the Good News addresses. This begins by examining what is sin.

We are taught from a young age that disobeying the law, especially biblical law, is sin. As good Christian parents, one of the very first things we teach our children is the

Ten Commandments. The Ten Commandments was given by God to Moses after He brought His chosen people out of bondage as described in the book of Exodus. Before this, the only commandment given by God recorded in the Old Testament was the one given to Adam in the Garden of Eden not to eat of a certain tree.

Of course, even in the earliest times referred to in Genesis, there were social laws established by man which allowed for the rise of civilizations and governed how men were to treat one another. None of these laws were given directly by God, though. Men saw order was necessary in order for them to join together peacefully and work in unity. Men also used certain social laws as a way to dominate their fellow man. Government was a shared dominion or stewardship, but there was always one person who had absolute authority over the people and who reaped the greatest benefit.

So, if sin is defined by God's law, how did God see man's wickedness before His commandments were given so that He had to bring the flood to wipe out their sin? Was sin defined by and restricted to His commandment or man's laws? Or was it something deeper than simple disobedience to the established spiritual or secular laws of their times? To answer that question, we need to look closely at what actually transpired when Adam and Eve disobeyed God.

> Now the serpent was more subtle than any beast of the field which the LORD God had made. And they said unto the woman, Yea, hath God said, Ye shall not eat of every tree of the garden? And the woman

said unto the serpent, We may eat of the fruit of the trees of the garden: But of the fruit of the tree which *is* in the midst of the garden, God hath said, Ye shall not eat of it, neither shall ye touch it, lest ye die. And the serpent said unto the woman, Ye shall not surely die: For God doth know that in the day ye eat thereof, then your eyes shall be opened, and ye shall be as gods, knowing good and evil. And when the woman saw that the tree *was* good for food, and that it *was* pleasant to the eyes, and a tree to be desired to make *one* wise, she took of the fruit thereof, and did eat, and gave also unto her husband with her; and they did eat. And the eyes of them both were opened, and they knew that they were naked; and they sewed fig leaves together, and made themselves aprons. And they heard the voice of the LORD God walking in the garden in the cool of the day: and Adam and their wife hid themselves from the presence of the LORD God amongst the trees of the garden.
Genesis 3:1-8

We often think the first sin was eating a piece of fruit from the Tree of the Knowledge of Good and Evil in the midst of the Garden of Eden and that somehow this piece of fruit had the power to corrupt man, separate him from God, and condemn him to Hell. We assume this fruit was evil and able to poison the soul of man immediately and for generations forever. However, the Bible is clear that God is not the author of evil and that all He created was good in His sight. We must conclude, therefore, that the fruit Adam and Eve ate was not evil in and of itself. The sin was not in the tree or in the fruit of the tree but in the act of disobedience to God and the desire for something apart from God.

God created man to have a free will, meaning the
ability to choose for himself what he wished to do.
God's full will for man was (and still is) beyond our
comprehension. God's will, as expressed in the first few
chapters of Genesis, was for man to exercise dominion
over all life in the earth and to nourish that which
God had given into his care. He was to be caretaker of
life on earth. However, God's plan extends far beyond
giving man the responsibility to care for the earth. As
revealed in Christ, a large part of His plan was for man
to become His children.

Adam and Eve both knew a small part of God's will
was for them to refrain from eating the fruit of one
particular tree in the Garden of Eden. It is likely that
tree was the same as all the other trees in terms of
wholesomeness of the fruit. It probably had no special
characteristic other than that God chose one tree out
of the many to use to see if His human creations would
remain submitted to His will. It was man who decided
he wanted to do something different from what God
required him to do.

We can speculate about the motivation of Adam and
Eve that led them to their fateful decision. Perhaps
Adam and Eve wanted to be like God in that God was
subject to no one. Perhaps they thought the fruit
would give them the same knowledge and power God
had. The idea of being able to gain knowledge from a
source outside of God Himself must have been new
and intriguing to them. God frequently spent the cool
hours of the morning strolling through the Garden

with Adam, in an intimate relationship with Adam, imparting knowledge of Himself to Adam. God was even working in fellowship with Adam, bringing the animals to him to name and teaching him the basics of language, all under His direction. God was literally the source of all knowledge for Adam and Eve.

As children are not able to learn everything their parents know in a short time, Adam and Eve could not have learned all that God knew even if they had millennia to walk with Him. The serpent deceitfully offered a shortcut to knowledge that, in the end, only taught one terrible lesson: that the wonderful relationship they had with God could be lost by disobeying God's one simple commandment.

Even before their act of disobedience, we can see the spirit of religion manifesting in Eve's response to the serpent's question in Genesis 3:3: "God hath said, Ye shall not eat of it, *neither shall ye touch it,* lest ye die." Although this was not an act of disobedience in that there was no command against this in their time, it was an indication to the serpent of what he could exploit to bring forth their downfall. In this case, the spirit of religion is shown when Eve responded with her own interpretation of God's commandment instead of simply responding with God's commandment exactly as He gave it. The Bible warns against adding our understanding to the Word of God in the book of Revelation 22:18-19 KJV: "For I testify unto every man that heareth the words of the prophecy of this book, If any man shall add unto these things, God shall add

unto him the plagues that are written in this book:
And if any man shall take away from the words of the
book of this prophecy, God shall take away his part out
of the book of life, and out of the holy city, and *from* the
things which are written in this book."

Although this admonition refers directly to the
spiritual truths imparted in the book of Revelation,
we should always commit what we share with others
to the Holy Spirit so we do not add error or confusion
to the message of the Good News.

In Revelation, God reveals there is a consequence to
adding anything to His word. By adding an additional
constraint to what God had commanded, Eve exercised
her will outside of God's will. This was the toehold the
tempter needed to argue his case with Adam and Eve.
The temptation was for them to gain knowledge apart
from the revelation of God. The knowledge promised
by the serpent and the knowledge delivered by the
serpent were two different things. The promise was
so vague it could have meant anything. The knowledge
given was that there was a horrible consequence to
their disobedience: spiritual death.

The nature of sin is this: knowing what God's will is
and choosing your own will instead. By giving man
free will, God gave man a choice between submitting
to God's divine nature or submitting to his own carnal
nature. Our fallen nature is evident in our predilection
to choose our will over His will.

It is interesting to note that there was a second special
tree in the Garden of Eden: the Tree of Life. God did not

command them not to eat of that tree. Although the
focus of this passage is on the temptation to partake
of the Tree of the Knowledge of Good and Evil, there
was another option given to Adam and Eve. If they had
instead partaken of the Tree of Life, they would have
been sealed into eternal life, and they would no longer
have been tempted by the Tree of the Knowledge of
Good and Evil.

> And the LORD God said, Behold, the man is become as
> one of us, to know good and evil: and now, lest they put
> forth their hand, and take also of the tree of life, and
> eat, and live for ever: Therefore the LORD God sent
> them forth from the garden of Eden, to till the ground
> from whence they was taken. So they drove out the
> man; and they placed at the east of the garden of Eden
> cherubim, and a flaming sword which turned every
> way, to keep the way of the tree of life.
> **Genesis 3:22-24**

The choice of Adam and Eve, the exercise of their will,
separated them from communion or fellowship with
God. Had they chosen the Tree of Life first, they would
have been sealed into an eternal relationship with God
possessing a divine nature. Should they have eaten of
the Tree of Life after first eaten from the Tree of the
Knowledge of Good and Evil, it would have sealed them
out of the possibility of having a relationship with
God at any point as they would have been locked into
an eternal life of disobedience, possessing only their
fallen nature. They were cast out of the Garden of Eden
for this reason only: so they would not eat of the Tree
of Life in their fallen condition. In Revelation 2:7b,

"To him that overcometh will I give to eat of the tree of life, which is in the midst of the paradise of God." The Tree of Life is still there as revealed in Revelation 22:2: "In the midst of the street of it, and on either side of the river, was there the tree of life, which bare twelve manner of fruits, and yielded her fruit every month: and the leaves of the tree were for the healing of the nations."

So, man's free will was the basis for their disobedience and of their separation from God. Free will could have been the basis for man's everlasting obedience and union with God. Man chose knowledge over knowing God. It has been this way since the fall of Adam and continues to this day. Even those who are religious concentrate on teaching what is good and what is evil as defined by the law of Moses, continuing to partake of the Tree of the Knowledge of Good and Evil and sharing it with their congregations. Instead, the church should be teaching that the veil of our fallen nature has been parted through the sacrifice of Christ and that we now have access to the presence of God so we may enter into a beautiful, restored relationship with Him. (I will discuss the veil in greater depth later in the book.)

Sadly, the only ones who could truly understand the consequences of their disobedience were Adam and Eve. They were the only ones who truly knew God, walking with Him daily in fellowship. They were the only ones who experienced life in the Garden of Eden and knew the difference between life with God and life without God. We cannot know the difference without first experiencing what it is to walk in fellowship with God. That experience was not possible for us until God Himself chose to bridge the gap by being made flesh and opening the way to a restored relationship with Him. It is only possible now by accepting Christ's sacrifice and God's invitation to that restored relationship with Him.

The bad news is that we have been separated from fellowship with God and we do not even know what we are missing. The good news is that God chose to do that which we could not do. He chose to pay the price for our disobedience and open the way for us to have a real relationship with Him. We once again have the opportunity to choose between doing His will or doing our own will. We can become co-laborers with the Holy Spirit to bring the knowledge of God into the spirits of those within the church who do not understand the true scope of the Good News so they also may truly live again in His presence.

Our sin nature has an enormous impact in keeping us in the darkness and in bondage. The consequences of our sin are innumerable and create a powerful barrier in the path of truth. I suggest it is wise to consider these consequences in the hope we can learn to overcome them through the Word.

Consequences

The majority of the Old Testament tells of the consequences of the fall of man and of man's attempt to return to God through his own efforts. It also reveals that God had a plan in place to restore man to Him by way of His promise to send a Savior. The consequences of the fall of man are too many to detail all of their effects in one chapter, but let us look at some of the more serious consequences of our separation from God.

SIN NATURE

The birth of our sin nature is immediately apparent in the actions of Adam and Eve. This was the first creative act of man apart from God. Instantly upon eating the fruit of the Tree of the Knowledge of Good and Evil, Adam and Eve became aware they were naked and called it evil. Perhaps they considered the obvious differences between male and female as evil and tried to hide those differences from view by making aprons of fig leaves. Nakedness was not a sin in God's eyes, but it was in man's eyes. This is the kind of knowledge that comes from the Tree of the Knowledge of Good and Evil. This was not knowledge given by God. It was, and continues to be, a false knowledge. Wearing clothes was not a commandment of God. God did not see their nakedness as sin. It was their new sin nature that convinced the pair that nakedness was evil.

A division was immediately evident between God's view of what was good and man's point of view. Before the fall, evil did not exist in God's creation. It was introduced by the will of man. It is true that the serpent tempted man, but he did not introduce evil into the world. Man invited evil into the world and began to define it in detail.

FEAR

Perhaps the greatest consequence of the fall of man is fear. The fear we are speaking of here is not physical fear, which is a mechanism of the flesh to protect itself, but a spiritual fear that keeps us from doing what is right and good in the eyes of God. In the Garden of Eden, there was no reason to fear, either in the physical sense or in the spiritual sense, since there were no physical dangers present and they were spiritually secure in God's presence.

The first thing Adam and Eve did once they ate of the fruit of the Tree of the Knowledge of Good and Evil was to flee from God and hide. First, they hid their bodies because they suddenly "knew" they were naked. Then they attempted to hide themselves from God's presence. Of course, it is impossible to hide from God, yet they tried out of fear.

Even though they had disobeyed God's command, God still looked for them in the Garden. It was not that God had not yet discovered their sin. God is omniscient and knows what will happen before it happens. He knew what the couple would decide before He spoke the words that created light. God wanted to give Adam and Eve the opportunity to again exercise their free will and confess and repent their disobedience. Instead, Adam and Eve blamed each other and gave excuses as though they could somehow justify themselves. They no longer saw themselves as justified by their relationship with God.

Their new sin nature impacted them immediately, and has continue to us now. Disobedience creates a sense of defenselessness in us because we know we are guilty and subject to the consequences of our action. Our fallen nature has two defensive responses: fight or flight. We hope to escape the consequences of our decisions or at least postpone them. We search for loopholes in what God said in the hope that what we did really wasn't bad and therefore not subject to punishment.

A third possible response Adam and Eve could have chosen was neither offensive nor defensive but rather submissive. Repentance and reconciliation with God, seeking pardon and restoration, is not based on fear. This is part of our divine nature, the nature which our fallen nature suppresses in us. Repentance and reconciliation are the will of God for us. Adam and Eve did not seem able to perceive this third response was available. Perhaps fear was such a new and powerful emotion to them that they reacted without thinking. The common response to fear is to react instead of to act.

It is important to understand that man's disobedience separated man from God but did not separate God from man. Our disobedience did not and cannot change God's love for us. God's love is evidenced in His providing suitable clothes for Adam and Eve before He expelled them from the Garden. The world outside of the Garden was not a paradise. It required effort to survive, and God provided protection from the elements out of His continued love for them.

God clothed Adam and Eve with the skins of the animals He created and placed under man's dominion. In effect, the first blood sacrifice was made by God for man's protection. This is a foreshadowing of the sacrifice He would make for us through Jesus. The sacrifices man offered to God throughout history were never sufficient. Indeed, they never could be sufficient because they were given selfishly, to somehow escape condemnation for their sin.

Second Timothy 1:7 reveals that God has not given us the spirit of fear: "For God hath not given us the spirit of fear; but of power, and of love, and of a sound mind." Rather, fear comes from our fallen nature. In the beginning, fear drove us from God. God always wanted us to walk in power and in love with a sound mind knowing Him and not fearing Him. When we see the word "fear" with respect to God in the Bible, it usually refers to awe and reverence of God; not terror of Him. "There is no fear in love; but perfect love casteth out fear: because fear hath torment. He that feareth is not made perfect in love" (1 John 4:18).

Fear is the antithesis of love. Where there is fear, love has no power. Where there is love, fear has no power. Fear delivers torment but love provides peace. When we experience God's love in His presence, we can no longer fear Him. Instead, as His children, we are able to draw near to Him and know His loving embrace. We can figuratively sit in His lap and listen to Him speaking to us of His love and of His wonderful plans for us. Those who know God love Him with everything they have, with everything they are. They desire to draw close to God, to develop an intimate and deep relationship with Him. Fear is no longer in those who enter into His presence. Children do not fear their Father. They love Him.

Fear has its own consequences: anger and hate. Anger is a product of our insecurity. We get angry because we do not feel things are happening in the way we want them to happen. We fear failure. We want to be in control. We want our will to be done. Captive of this anger, we support other people if their will does not conflict with our own. We hate others whose will conflicts with ours. We blame others for our failures and weaknesses. Especially, we hate God whose will is often counter to our will. We will even go so far as to deny God's existence to justify getting what we want.

When we come to know God, we start to realize we have never been in control nor ever can be. We begin to comprehend we are only one very small influence in the state of things. When we join with others, certainly our influence can grow, but it never becomes absolute.

When we submit our will to God's will, we find God's will has always been for our good, and we begin to enjoy our own total lack of control. We no longer need to be angry. We no longer hate. We can just enjoy His presence and rest in His direction.

SPIRITUAL AND PHYSICAL DEATH

In Genesis 2:17, God tells Adam he will surely die if he eats of the fruit of the Tree of the Knowledge of Good and Evil. Most believe this refers to our physical bodies and point to man's decline in lifespan as time passed from the expulsion. The truth is that the immediate consequence of eating that fruit was a spiritual death evidenced by the immediate breaking of man's fellowship with God and ending in man's expulsion from the Garden of Eden. The resulting decline in the longevity of the physical body is an indirect consequence of our separation from the presence of God. The source of all life is God. To be cut off from that source is to slowly die of starvation of the life-giving presence of God.

In Christ, we are born again. The veil of our fallen nature is parted and no longer able to keep us from God's presence. Although we still possess a fallen nature, Jesus made a way past it into the presence of God. We have access to new life in Him, and that life manifests as we draw ever closer in relationship to Him. It is in His presence we receive healing. It is in His presence we are delivered from our addictions. In

His presence, temptations lose their hold over us. We come to know His voice and His love for us. As Christ is revealed in us, we enter into the process of becoming the sons of God, being transformed into the image and likeness of Jesus Christ. Death no longer abides in us but rather abundant life manifests in us and touches those around us.

DISEASE

Pathogens, which are the cause of disease, are a consequence of the corruption of the earth. The serpent has been able to corrupt the earth continually because man has not been a good steward of it. The serpent was never given dominion over the earth, but by manipulating man's sin nature, it is able to use man to sow corruption within it. Often, the serpent uses the greed of man to corrupt, whether it is greed for knowledge or greed for worldly profit. As the serpent corrupts man, it corrupts all that man was given dominion over. Indifference, fear, hate, and other human weaknesses are used by the serpent to sow discord and corruption. God gave man dominion over every living thing to care for it, but man has not properly exercised that dominion because of his separation from God. Our ability to exercise dominion depends on our submission to another's will. Are we submitted to God's will or to the will of the powers and principalities of this world?

"Submit yourselves therefore to God. Resist the devil, and he will flee from you. Draw nigh to God, and he will draw nigh to you. Cleanse your hands, ye sinners; and purify your hearts, ye double minded" **(James 4:7-8)**.

As we submit to God, our ability to properly exercise our dominion returns to us. We can resist the devil's temptation to walk in the flesh and restore to proper function that which has been corrupted. We cannot be double-minded, believing the lie that there is nothing we can do. We must turn away from the ways we used to do things and look to God for direction in how to exercise godly dominion. Through Christ's sacrifice, we can draw near to God and work with God to restore that which was lost or corrupted.

"No man can enter into a strong man's house, and spoil his goods, except he will first bind the strong man; and then he will spoil his house" **(Mark 3:27)**.

In the Garden, the serpent bound the strong man (Adam) with sin. He spoiled Adam's house (the world) and became the strong man himself. Through Jesus victory, that strong man (Satan) is now bound and we can enter his house (the world) and reclaim all he has stolen from us. The church, composed of everyone who follows Christ, will destroy the gates of hell and enter into the victory Jesus won for us.

"And I say also unto thee, That thou art Peter, and upon this rock I will build my church; and the gates of hell shall not prevail against it" **(Matt. 16:18)**.

DOMINION

As I've stated, God gave man dominion over every living thing in the earth. This dominion was not taken from man in the fall but was distorted and corrupted through the fallen nature of man. The serpent does not operate directly in the world, but tempts man to do his bidding.

> And God said, Let us make man in our image, after our likeness: and let them have dominion over the fish of the sea, and over the fowl of the air, and over the cattle, and over all the earth, and over every creeping thing that creepeth upon the earth. So God created man in his own image, in the image of God created he him; male and female created he them. And God blessed them, and God said unto them, Be fruitful, and multiply, and replenish the earth, and subdue it: and have dominion over the fish of the sea, and over the fowl of the air, and over every living thing that moveth upon the earth. **Genesis 1:26-28**

The first thing we need to realize from this passage is that man was given dominion over every living thing except for one: himself. God has always reserved dominion over man for Himself. As we examine God's Word, we see the results of man's unreasoning desire to exercise dominion in ways God never intended. Wars have raged throughout history due to man's desire to dominate other men. Man continues to this day attempting to exercise dominion over all men whom God has reserved to Himself.

"Unto the woman he said, I will greatly multiply thy sorrow and thy conception; in sorrow thou shalt bring forth children; and thy desire *shall* be to thy husband, and he shall rule over thee" **(Gen. 3:16)**.

Man was not given dominion over woman either. Due to her sin nature, which is no different than man's sin nature, God revealed to Eve that her desire will be for her husband. Man was given authority over woman as a consequence of the fall, but he was not given dominion. In this way, woman's relationship with man would be an example of man's relationship with God and man's desire for God. As Eve's desire was for Adam, so has man's desire been throughout history for God. As Adam's authority was over Eve, so has God's authority over man been expressed throughout time. God's dominion over man requires man's submission to Him but His authority is not based on man's willing submission.

And unto Adam he said, Because thou hast hearkened unto the voice of thy wife, and hast eaten of the tree, of which I commanded thee, saying, Thou shalt not eat of it: cursed is the ground for thy sake; in sorrow shalt thou eat *of* it all the days of thy life; Thorns also and thistles shall it bring forth to thee; and thou shalt eat the herb of the field; In the sweat of thy face shalt thou eat bread, till thou return unto the ground; for out of it wast thou taken: for dust thou *art*, and unto dust shalt thou return. **Genesis 3:17-19**

Please notice that God did not curse the ground out of spite. The ground was cursed for a purpose in response to man's disobedience. Refusing to submit to God's will effectively separates man from God's blessing. Man's dominion over the earth was, and is, contingent upon God having dominion over man. If we look at the world system around us, it's evident all authority is given by a higher power. It is limited by that higher authority and cannot exceed the level of authority of that higher power. For example, we can only function in our jobs based on the limits of authority we are given. Our bosses are also limited in the authority they can exercise by their bosses, so on and so forth. Governments exist because of God's authority, but they exist corruptly because they are not submitted to God's dominion.

So, why did God give man dominion over every living thing that moved on the earth? For the reason that God wanted man to be the caretakers of this world. Submitted to God, man was to care for this world in the same manner that God intended to care for man—with love. Instead of being submitted to God's intent, man has exploited the world for his own purposes, namely greed and power.

In man's pursuit of dominion over their fellow man, he has used creativity to invent ever more powerful means to exercise that corrupted dominion. The resources of this world have been used to create more efficient ways to kill and destroy, to create civilizations for the purpose of exercising dominion over peoples, and to invent new ways to extend man's dominion. Instead of caring for the world, mankind has polluted it, extracting its minerals and burning its forests. Waste pollutes the ocean. Whole species of life are now extinct; the life God gave into mankind's care to cherish and protect. Though all that mankind has created from the knowledge of good and evil is used for both good and evil, for the majority of mankind has only looked to how it can benefit from its actions and not to the consequences of those actions.

It is not the intent of this book to judge man. God is our judge. However, it must be pointed out that there are consequences to our separation from God. We do not walk in the knowledge of God but in our limited knowledge derived from our understanding of the world around us. We stumble about forever seeking knowledge but are unable to anticipate all the consequences of acting on that knowledge because man's knowledge is always incomplete. Scientific theories describe the world around us in approximations but only the Creator truly knows His creation. We can only experiment, theorize, and speculate. We create seemingly marvelous things with our knowledge, but it always comes at a cost to the world we live in.

On the other hand, the knowledge of God cannot be used for evil. Through knowing Him, submitting to Him, and working with Him as co-laborers in caring for the world, we can restore the earth to the paradise He intended it to be. We can become the children of God according to His original purpose and plan. Unfortunately, unless all mankind repents and returns to God, corruption will remain in this earth. Yet God does promise a new earth to those who seek Him. Jesus will return in His glory and the evil mankind has loosed will be done away with.

So, we can see our separation from God has consequences not only in us but in all that we touch. The promise of God is that, as we are restored to Him, fear and death lose their power over us. As we submit to our Father's dominion, our dominion over this world can also be restored to us in the way it was meant to be.

Mankind Walking Alone

In chapter 4 of the book of Genesis, we find the beginnings of man's struggle to walk without fellowship with God. Adam and Eve brought only three things out of the Garden of Eden: the fruit of the Tree of the Knowledge of Good and Evil, the clothes made for them by God, and the memory of walking with God. They could no longer walk in the knowledge that God shared with them daily but instead had to rely on the knowledge gained from experience and interpreted by their limited understanding.

God did warn them they would need to work hard to survive instead of enjoying the rest that comes in His presence. In the Garden of Eden, man worked with God under God's direction and the work was easy. For instance, God brought the animals to Adam to see what he would name them. I can picture Adam sitting at ease in the Garden while God did all the hard work of finding and bringing the animals to him. Of course, this was not hard for God to do but you can see if God had instructed Adam to seek out all the animals and name them, the task would have been close to impossible. In fact, the task continues to this day with scientists seeking out new species of animals and plants to name and study. When we work with God, the tasks He gives are easy for us because He designed us with the capabilities to do them. He reserves for Himself the care of those things we find impossible.

The world outside the Garden of Eden was harsh and unforgiving. Many dangers surrounded the first people, and mistakes could kill. In order to survive without God's help, men had to learn how to gather fruit, which was no longer as abundant as in the Garden, and to add roots and vegetables to their diet while avoiding those that were poisonous. In order to clothe themselves from the elements, they had to learn to hunt animals for their fur. The weather was harsh with freezing cold in the winter and unpredictable storms to endure. Rain was not always reliable, and water often become scarce. Many animals were now quite deadly, and they had to learn to either hide from them or somehow protect themselves. They learned to use fire for protection during the night, for warmth during the cold, and to cook meat to further stave off hunger. Animal bones and sinew were used to make tools and weapons to aid survival. Men took shelter wherever they could and learned to make shelter when they could not find any.

It was all a dramatic change from life in the Garden. Instead of walking in the dominion God had given them over the earth, they began walking in a distorted dominion based on the knowledge from the Tree of the Knowledge of Good and Evil. Though God had given them dominion over life on earth, in this new world they redefined this dominion in terms of their own survival and what they perceived as beneficial for them alone.

As men began to understand the world around them, they learned how to control their environment. Scavenging to survive was hard work and not always sufficient since animals were competing for the same resources. Men eventually found there were animals they could trap, domesticate, and harvest without putting themselves in danger by hunting. The herding of animals is the one activity that most closely matches God's original intent for man to care for this world. Perhaps this is why Jesus referred to Himself as a pastor of sheep. Even so, herding was distorted to the benefit of mankind rather than to better fulfil the command of God to care for life. People herd animals for their skins, their milk, their wool, their meat, and so on, all for their benefit. Shepherds care for animals not because the animals need their protection but so that they may profit from them.

People also found they could plant seeds and harvest fruit without roaming the land looking for naturally-growing fruits, vegetables, and grains. Farming provided them with the means to settle down in one place and supply the needs of a larger group of people. But farming also depended on things they could not control, such as the weather and other animals who also wanted to eat the crops. This led to inventing irrigation to water the fields and fences to protect their crops. Since men no longer wandered far in search of food, they had to build permanent shelters where the land was fertile. Yet while farming sounds good, it also led to the destruction of forests and the creatures God created to live there. Instead of enjoying the fruits provided freely by God's natural world, men chopped down the forests to plant crops so they could have more while working less. Certainly, remaining in one place beat wandering the forests in search for food and shelter, however it is an example of how men have ever looked to making things easier for themselves without considering the consequences on the life around them.

As they struggled to survive, men discovered they could also use the minerals and metals in the ground and stones of the land around them. They learned how to dig into the earth and to process what they found into useful tools and weapons. Sharp stones became weapons to hunt with and tools with which to harvest skins and meat. Mining and metalworking increased men's ability to survive, and they began inventing ways to extract harder metals, such as copper and iron, for greater gain. They invented methods to make stronger tools and weapons. Over time, they created ever more powerful weapons to use against each other and over the world.

Learning to mine minerals and metals also allowed them to delve into the earth and seek the riches lying there. They began to attribute value to stones and metals, counting them as riches so valuable as to justify killing for. Nations began fighting wars over these and other resources. Men twisted the knowledge they had won over the years in inventing all manner of things and used it, and those many inventions, to kill each other and bring ever more destruction upon the world given into their care.

People soon exercised their creativity inventing industries, such as textiles, shipbuilding, and the crafts and arts. They built cities to live in. Civilizations rose and fell. Fear ruled the world with no restraint because men no longer considered God first. All that mattered was maintaining their power even at the expense of the survival of those around them. Over time, as they drew even further from God, they became destroyers of the world. Their greed increased and they were overcome with pride. They ridiculed the few remaining who still looked for God.

What mankind considers as good is usually perceived as good only in terms of what is considered good for mankind. Following this course of history of mankind walking alone without God, what was good for the life of the world that was given into man's care was lost in the struggle.

God looked upon the wickedness of man and knew it could not continue without people totally destroying themselves along with the world God created for them. To deal with their wickedness and to save the world, God needed to destroy His highest creation—mankind. He sent a flood to wipe the earth clean of mankind's sin, but He chose to save one man who was still seeking to follow God: Noah. Even though Noah was obedient in building the ark, he was not perfect; he was also a sinner. God had to spare his wife and children and their wives as well if man was to continue in the world. However, since his wife and children were not seeking God as Noah was, sin continued in the world.

TRYING TO RETURN TO GOD

"And the woman said unto the serpent, We may eat of the fruit of the trees of the garden: But of the fruit of the tree which is in the midst of the garden, God hath said, Ye shall not eat of it, neither shall ye touch it, lest ye die" **(Gen. 3:2-3)**.

Religion is the invention of mankind. We saw its beginning in Eve's reply to the serpent. When responding to the tempter, Eve added *"neither shall ye touch it"* (emphasis mine) to God's command. Wasn't it enough to simply declare what God said without adding to it? Thankfully, when Jesus was likewise tempted in the wilderness, as related in Matthew 4:1-10, He responded only with "It is written" and quoted the Word of God. He did not argue with the tempter nor did He add His own interpretation to the Word.

Throughout the Old Testament, mankind has added their understanding to what God has said in an attempt to return to what was lost; walking with God in fellowship in the Garden of Eden. This started with Eve's children, Cain and Abel. They attempted to return to God by their own actions. Cain and Abel did not have direct experience of the Garden of Eden's paradise but they must have heard stories of it from

Adam and Eve. Cain and Abel decided to bring an offering to God of their labors even though there is no biblical evidence that God requested an offering. It is not clear what motivated the brothers to bring the offering. Perhaps they thought they could influence God to let them into the Garden of Eden so they could experience it themselves. Whatever the reason, they performed an act of man-made religion. Anything we do that God has not asked us to do is an act of religion and is not born out of a personal relationship with Him.

God saw in one of the offerings a reflection of His plan to restore man to a personal relationship with Him. It was the offering of a blood sacrifice. God respected that offering more than the other only because it foreshadowed the sacrifice of the Christ. Cain, in the pride of his being the firstborn, was angry with God for not favoring his sacrifice. That anger led to the first murder recorded in the Bible—fratricide. Cain and Abel's intentions did not have the result they hoped for.

As we go through the Old Testament, we find it does not just record history, but also reveals both the character of God and the character of mankind. Mankind continued trying to exercise its own idea of what dominion should be. Men repeatedly tried to use what God said to justify themselves or their actions. One example is found in Genesis 4:23-24 where a man named Lamech confessed to killing two men who had hurt him. He used God's declaration that Cain would be avenged sevenfold if anyone slew him to declare that he himself would be avenged seventy and sevenfold for anyone trying to avenge the murders he had committed. What God had judged for Cain was intended to be specific to Cain. God had not pronounced judgment on Lamech yet Lamech claimed Cain's case as reason to be protected from the consequence of his actions. Lawyers call this a defense based on a legal precedent. It appears that legalism came even before Mosaic law was given. The problem with Lamech's idea is that God's judgment is perfect and very specific to the situation He addresses. Cain's punishment resulted in his being banished for life from the society he lived in. Lamech's intention was to simply escape punishment for his actions by the society he lived in.

God's law was not given to the chosen people until their deliverance from Egypt. The law was simple. There were only ten commandments. All of the rest of the law of Moses was based on man's interpretation of God's law and of other instructions God gave them. Religion is based on men's interpretation of God's intent as seen through the imperfect lens of their own fallen nature.

We do not need to trace in detail the progress of religion through man's interpretation of the law and of the covenants throughout the Old Testament. The many books of the Old Testament trace the history of God's offering to reestablish His relationship with His children and of men's insistence in doing their own thing.

The Old Testament shows the evolution of religion over time as men continued to redefine for themselves who God was and what His law meant. Mankind even went so far as to invent other gods to take the place of God. These were gods formed of their own hands to represent the things they could not understand or control. These false gods had no power, but the serpent used them to lead the people even further from God.

Religion soon became a means to control people. Priests lived off of the sacrifices of others and invented even more laws to tighten their grip over those who put their trust in the god or gods the priests represented. Religion was even used to control kingdoms, requiring priests' blessings to anoint and appoint kings and queens.

Over and over in the Old Testament, we see mankind attempting to return to God. but these attempts invariably are corrupted by a desire for political power and/or wealth. This continues to this day as we can see in current world politics.

God's Promise

Even though mankind continued to insist on walking in this world according to their own will and understanding, God prepared them to fulfill the promise He made in the book of Genesis 3:14-15: "And the LORD God said unto the serpent, Because thou hast done this, thou art cursed above all cattle, and above every beast of the field; upon thy belly shalt thou go, and dust shalt thou eat all the days of thy life. And I will put enmity between thee and the woman, and between thy seed and her seed; he shall bruise thy head, and thou shalt bruise his heel."

It is interesting to note this promise was not made to Adam, nor to Eve, but to the serpent. This is the promise of God: to provide an opponent to the tempter from the seed of the woman. Though this passage refers to the woman having seed, the man is actually the source of seed in nature and woman provides the egg to be fertilized by the seed. A woman can provide seed only though giving birth to a male child. The promised opponent must therefore be a man.

God's promise in this passage was to provide a man, the seed of Eve, who would stand firm against the tempter and his temptation and succeed where Adam and Eve had failed. This is the first word of hope given by God to encourage fallen mankind to believe that a way back to the Father would be provided to them. The only evidence in Genesis that there were men who walked upright before God were Enoch and Elijah. Genesis 5:22 tells us Enoch walked with God for 300 years after fathering Methuselah before God took him. God fell silent about his promise until mankind became so corrupt that violence ruled. When He decided to destroy mankind with a flood, there was only one man left who was upright before Him. God spoke only to Noah to build an ark to save his family. Without Noah to provide the lineage, God could not fulfill His promise to Adam and Eve.

Everyone in the Old Testament looked forward to the day that God's promise would be fulfilled. However, in all of the Old Testament, not one man or woman was successful in resisting the temptation to put their will before God's will, including Enoch, Noah, and Elijah.

Theologians equate the serpent in Genesis to a spiritual entity called Satan. This particular spiritual entity is identified as the opponent of God's creation and the accuser of mankind. The word translated "Satan" in the Old Testament literally means "an opponent or adversary." In the New Testament, the word translated "Satan" literally means "the accuser." Satan is not referred to as mankind's opponent in the New Testament because he was defeated by Jesus and can no longer oppose the children of the Living God without resistance. Instead, he stands as mankind's accuser before God and Jesus stands as the evidence that Satan's accusations no longer apply to God's children. Satan still tempts us, but with the help of the Holy Spirit, we have the ability to resist that temptation.

As a side note, another name theologians have attributed to Satan is "Lucifer".

How art thou fallen from heaven, O Lucifer, son of the morning! [how] art thou cut down to the ground, which didst weaken the nations! For thou hast said in thine heart, I will ascend into heaven, I will exalt my throne above the stars of God: I will sit also upon the mount of the congregation, in the sides of the north: I will ascend above the heights of the clouds; I will be like the most High. Yet thou shalt be brought down to hell, to the sides of the pit. **Isaiah 14:12-15**

The word lucifer means "shining one" or "bringer of light." Theological thinking postulates that this is a description of an archangel who was cast out of heaven and took a third of the angels with him, these becoming the devils spoken about in the scriptures. However, Satan being cast out of heaven is a future event as detailed in the book of Revelations. Therefore, Lucifer cannot be another name for Satan.

And there was war in heaven: Michael and his angels fought against the dragon; and the dragon fought and his angels, And prevailed not; neither was their place found any more in heaven. And the great dragon was cast out, that old serpent, called the Devil, and Satan, which deceiveth the whole world: he was cast out into the earth, and his angels were cast out with him. And I heard a loud voice saying in heaven, Now is come salvation, and strength, and the kingdom of our God, and the power of his Christ; for the accuser of our brethren is cast down, who accused them before our God day and night. **Revelations 12:7-10**

However, if Isaiah 14:12-15 is taken in context, it is more likely the name Lucifer refers to a particular king of Babylon. The name Lucifer can be applied to all who willfully and consciously exalt themselves over God. As shown in Isaias 15, the destiny of any man who tries to exalt himself as greater than God will be cast down and abased. We also see this in the book of Daniel where we encounter a king of Babylon by the name of Nebuchadnezzar. He erected a golden statue of himself and commanded all the people to bow down and worship him. Shadrach, Meshach, and Abednego refused and were cast into a flaming furnace where they were delivered by God in the form of a man who appeared to Nebuchadnezzar as a son of the gods. In the end, this king was cast down by God for seven years to eat grass like an ox in the fields before being reinstated. Under his rule afterward, Babylon was restored and became known as "the city of light."

All men from Adam until now exalt themselves over God to some degree whenever they chose to do their own will rather than God's will. However, they do not necessarily do so consciously or intentionally. Most people simply do not know any better. Many Christians think they have an excuse by saying they do not know what God's will is. The Bible, along with the guidance of the Holy Spirit, was given to us so all could know and obey God's will, not just in general terms but also to know His specific will for our lives.

> Now there was a day when the sons of God came to present themselves before the Lord, and Satan came also among them. And the Lord said unto Satan, Whence comest thou? Then Satan answered the Lord, and said, From going to and fro in the earth, and from walking up and down in it. And the Lord said unto Satan, Hast thou considered my servant Job, that there is none like him in the earth, a perfect and an upright man, one that feareth God, and escheweth evil? Then Satan answered the Lord, and said, Doth Job fear God for nought? Hast not thou made an hedge about him, and about his house, and about all that he hath on every side? thou hast blessed the work of his hands, and his substance is increased in the land. But put forth thine hand now, and touch all that he hath, and he will curse thee to thy face. And the Lord said unto Satan, Behold, all that he hath is in thy power; only upon himself put not forth thine hand. So Satan went forth from the presence of the Lord. **Job 1:6-12**

In the book of Job, Satan is referred to as one of the sons of God. He is portrayed as standing before God to accuse mankind. He goes about the earth, walking up and down in it. Satan is the one who brings torment upon mankind, but he is limited in what he can do by God. His function seems to be to test mankind, and it is apparent he takes great delight in doing so. There is much speculation as to why God allows this. It may be related to the fact that the way someone exercises his or her free will cannot be revealed until it is tested. Will that person resist the temptation and remain submitted to God's will? In all of the Bible, only Jesus did not fall to Satan's temptation.

It is evident that mankind's tempter and accuser has been active in the earth since the very beginning of creation and will continue to be active until the final return of Jesus in victory. But we must remember that Jesus defeated him by refusing to succumb to temptation even unto the cross. His submission and obedience to God paid the price for our sin—past, present, and future. In response, the Father rent the veil in the Temple from top to bottom, opening the way for all mankind to enter into the Holy of Holies and into His very presence. We may not be able to naturally resist temptation due to our sin nature, but God made provision for us in Christ.

> And the Lord spake unto Moses, saying, Take the rod, and gather thou the assembly together, thou, and Aaron thy brother, and speak ye unto the rock before their eyes; and it shall give forth his water, and thou shalt bring forth to them water out of the rock: so thou shalt give the congregation and their beasts drink. And Moses took the rod from before the Lord, as he commanded him. And Moses and Aaron gathered the congregation together before the rock, and he said unto them, Hear now, ye rebels; must we fetch you water out of this rock? And Moses lifted up his hand, and with his rod he smote the rock twice: and the water came out abundantly, and the congregation drank, and their beasts also. And the Lord spake unto Moses and Aaron, Because ye

believed me not, to sanctify me in the eyes of the children of Israel, therefore ye shall not bring this congregation into the land which I have given them. **Numbers 20:7-12**

Throughout the Old Testament, the history of the chosen people reflects the successes and failures of their leaders. Every one of them fell to some temptation and failed to obey God in some manner or the other. Moses failed to obey God and struck the rock twice with the rod instead of just speaking to the rock for the water to flow. He was not allowed to enter the promised land because of his disobedience. David was an adulterer and murderer even though God called him a man after his own heart: "... he raised up unto them David to be their king; to whom also he gave their testimony, and said, I have found David the son of Jesse, a man after mine own heart, which shall fulfil all my will" (Acts 13:22). Solomon allowed altars to other gods in order to please his wives instead of striving to please God. As is reiterated in Romans 2:23: "For all have sinned, and come short of the glory of God."

There were those God used to speak to His chosen people and warn them of the sin they were committing. God spoke through the prophets about the Promised One. The prophets were those few people who could hear God's voice and pass on God's warnings and promises to the rest of the chosen people. Most people could not recognize His voice and therefore walked only by their understanding. Even though God's people had the laws of Moses, they did not have spiritual discernment to understand the truth. True prophets were scarce among the chosen people. Most of those who called themselves prophets were false prophets who only gave good "prophecies" to the people who paid them. In other words, they "prophesied" for their own gain.

Son of man, I have made thee a watchman unto the house of Israel: therefore hear the word at my mouth, and give them warning from me. When I say unto the wicked, Thou shalt surely die; and thou givest him not warning, nor speakest to warn the wicked from his wicked way, to save his life; the same wicked man shall die in his iniquity; but his blood will I require at thine hand. Yet if thou warn the wicked, and he turn not from his wickedness, nor from his wicked way, he shall die in his iniquity; but thou hast delivered thy soul. Again, When a righteous man doth turn from his righteousness, and commit iniquity, and I lay a stumbling-block before him, he shall die: because thou hast not given him warning, he shall die in his sin, and his righteousness which he hath done shall not be remembered; but his blood will I require at thine hand. Nevertheless if thou warn the righteous man, that the righteous sin not, and he doth not sin, he shall surely live, because he is warned; also thou hast delivered thy soul. **Ezekiel 3:17-21**

In this passage in Ezekiel, we see the purpose of a prophet was to serve as a watchman or guard who could cry out at the approach of danger. God's warning to Ezekiel to be faithful in fulfilling his duty as a prophet was serious enough to require repeating. A prophet who did not cry out the warning of God would be guilty of the blood of those who did not receive the warning.

Thus saith the Lord; Go down to the house of the king of Judah, and speak there this word, And say, Hear the word of the Lord, O king of Judah, that sittest upon the throne of David, thou, and thy servants, and thy people that enter in by these gates: Thus saith the Lord; Execute ye judgment and righteousness, and deliver the spoiled out of the hand of the oppressor: and do no wrong, do no violence to the stranger, the fatherless, nor the widow, neither shed innocent blood in this place. For if ye do this thing indeed, then shall there enter in by the gates of this house kings sitting upon the throne of David, riding in chariots and on horses, he, and his servants, and his people. But if ye will not hear these words, I swear by myself, saith the Lord, that this house shall become a desolation. **Jeremiah 22:1-5**

True prophets gave warnings from God. The passage above is an example of this. If those to whom the warning was given did not repent or turn away from what they were doing, very specific bad things would happen. If they did repent, then good things would happen. The prophecies or calls to repentance were not always directed to God's chosen people. An example of this is seen in Jonah's mission; he was sent to Nineveh to call those people to repentance. Jonah is also a good example of the imperfection of the messenger, first for trying to run away from the task and, second, for getting mad at God for showing mercy to Nineveh when its citizens repented.

The true prophets were able to recognize God's voice, one of their most important characteristics. Although all men are created with the ability to hear

God speaking, most people do not recognize which of the voices they hear in their thoughts is His voice. To do this requires an intimate knowledge of the Word and a life dedicated to meditating on that Word and seeking God. In the Old Testament, the Holy Spirit was not yet given to dwell within man but was present to speak to and through those who sought to hear from God. When God created Adam, He breathed His Spirit into him. This means we have a spirit which is able to connect with God and hear His voice. Unfortunately for many, that voice is all too often a still and quiet voice that can easily be drowned out by the loud voice of the flesh.

True prophets were hated by the rulers of the chosen people because they pointed out the sins these leaders were committing. In 1 Thessalonians 2:15, Paul refers to the Jewish leaders not only as killers of Jesus but also of the prophets. Although there are no direct references to the killing of prophets during the 400 years after Malachi, it is a possibility the religious leaders took to eliminating anyone who did not speak what they wanted to hear. Accusations of blasphemy merited death in their interpretation of Mosaic law, accusations they also brought against Jesus.

So, we can see that, beginning with the promise in Genesis that the Promised One would be born of a woman, the book of Genesis spells out Jesus's lineage. All of the prophets, from Isaias to Malachi, contributed to further defining the arrival of the Messiah, the Anointed One, even naming the town where He would be born. They described how He would be rejected by His people and crucified as a criminal, and they predicted His triumph over Satan and His ascension to the right hand of God. But even with all that, God's people were unable to recognize Him when He came into their midst. Their expectations of the Messiah were that He would be a king who would deliver them from Rome and restore the kingdom of Israel. They did not understand God's purpose was to restore mankind to fellowship with Him.

Prophecies in the Old Testament ceased with the prophet Malachi. There is a four-century gap between the book of Malachi and the New Testament. Most theologians believe that gap exists because God had nothing more to say. However, if you read the book of Malachi, you will see that Israel was no longer interested in hearing from God, preferring to perform an outward religious practice instead. As He makes clear in Malachi 1:2, God never stopped loving Israel. But Israel's heart was no longer toward God. God declares His people no longer honored Him in Malachi 1:6. The priest's offerings to the Lord were no longer of the best but were instead only given out of tradition. "Ye offer polluted bread upon mine altar; and ye say, Wherein have we polluted thee? In that ye say, The table of the Lord is contemptible. And if ye offer the blind for sacrifice, is it not evil? and if ye offer the lame and sick, is it not evil? offer it now unto thy governor; will he be pleased with thee, or accept thy person? saith the Lord of hosts." (Mal. 1:7-8) They did not expect to hear from God, and therefore were no longer listening for His voice.

Israel even stopped treating each other with honor. They began marrying people of other religions. They divorced their wives to marry outside of their religion. They no longer brought their tithes to the priests. They ignored the Ten Commandments in their pursuit of the things of this world. In effect, God was trying to speak to the deaf. And during this time, Israel was conquered, first by the Persians, then by the Greeks, and finally by Rome. When they turned their backs on God, God could no longer protect them.

The entirety of all the prophecies concerning the Messiah were no longer given credence. By the end of the Old Testament, God's promise had become a religious myth to most. But the day would finally come when the Promised One would be revealed, not just to the chosen people, but to the whole world.

The Appointed Time

Millennia after the fall, all mankind was able to do was adhere to their traditions, intellectual philosophies, doctrines, and theologies. The religious spent their time studying God's Word only to limit it to their understanding, adding ever demanding laws until it became an impossible burden on the people.

As the chosen people drew away from God, they divided themselves between the lands of Judah and of Israel around 931 BC. Then the Assyrians conquered Israel in 722 BC. and the Babylonians conquered Judah in 596 BC. This began the period of the Exile. Even when the chosen people returned from the Exile, they were still ruled by Babylon until it fell to the Persians in 529 BC. The Persians were conquered by Alexander the Great in 338 BC, and Rome conquered Jerusalem in 32 BC. Greek became the common language of Israel during their three hundred years as part of the Greek empire. In total, the chosen people had been in subjection to a series of conquerors for over 700 years before the appointed time arrived for God to fulfil His promise. They remained subject to other rulers until AD 1948 for a total of almost 2,650 years.

The political conditions of God's appointed time were tumultuous. Kings appointed by Rome ruled over Israel and Samaria. These kings were only interested in maintaining their power and cared little about God. The chosen people were still divided between the north and the south, with the Jews looking down on the Samaritans. Jewish government consisted of the Roman-appointed kings, who were only interested in maintaining Rome's power, and several religious groups. Civil law was enforced only by the Romans. Spiritual law was left to the Sanhedrin, the Jewish religious authority composed of religious leaders of the three major sects: the scribes, the Pharisees, and the Sadducees.

The scribes played a major role in the interpretation of scripture and in the formation of doctrine during the time between the beginning of the Exile and the destruction of the Temple in AD 70. Initially, they were responsible for creating legal documents and for making accurate copies of the books of the Old Testament but eventually were better known for their interpretation of the scriptures and for the development of religious doctrine. They were mostly aligned with the Pharisees doctrinally. In a word, they were Old Testament theologians. Besides the Ten Commandments of God and the Mosaic laws detailed in the Pentateuch, the scribes included oral traditions and Jewish customs in their development and interpretation of doctrine.

The most fervently religious were divided into various sects, among which were the Pharisees and

Sadducees. Many of the priests ascribed to these two sects, although some did not. Jesus's opinion of the Pharisees and scribes can be found throughout the four Gospels. His opinion is perhaps the clearest in Matthew 23 where He condemned their pride:

> Then spake Jesus to the multitude, and to his disciples, Saying, The scribes and the Pharisees sit in Moses' seat: All therefore whatsoever they bid you observe, that observe and do; but do not ye after their works: for they say, and do not. For they bind heavy burdens and grievous to be borne, and lay them on men's shoulders; but they themselves will not move them with one of their fingers. But all their works they do for to be seen of men: they make broad their phylacteries, and enlarge the borders of their garments, And love the uppermost rooms at feasts, and the chief seats in the synagogues, And greetings in the markets, and to be called of men, Rabbi, Rabbi. But be not ye called Rabbi: for one is your Master, even Christ; and all ye are brethren. And call no man your father upon the earth: for one is your Father, which is in heaven. Neither be ye called masters: for one is your Master, even Christ. But he that is greatest among you shall be your servant. And whosoever shall exalt himself shall be abased; and he that shall humble himself shall be exalted. **Matthew 23:1-12**

In this chapter of Matthew, we see all the hallmarks of religion. Those in authority defined the requirements to be accepted into the group and looked down on any who could not meet their standards.

Jesus said the scribes and Pharisees sat in Moses's seat. That means they were the official interpreters of the law of Moses for the chosen people. Please note, Jesus did not dispute their interpretation but rather that they did not do what they wanted everyone else to do. Perhaps you have heard the expression "Do what I say, not what I do"?

In Matthew 23:7-10 there is a warning against pride; pride in having titles and positions and in exalting others by calling them your master or father. The New Testament details the different functions within the church, but religion turns those functions into titles that highlight the title holder as superior to the common believer because of a degree or because they are ordained by other men. Yet Jesus declared there is only one Master for us, Christ, and only one Father, God.

Jesus clearly detailed in Matthew 23:13-39 all the things the religious did that illustrated their hypocrisy and the evil they were committing against the chosen people. These authorities relished their positions before men and profited from them. Yet they committed injustices by their interpretation of the law. In Matthew 23:13, Jesus stated they made the law to be a burden to the people, thereby not permitting them to enter the kingdom of God and, at the same time, declining to enter the kingdom themselves. The religious leaders blocked the way of repentance and restoration to God by standing against John the Baptist and Jesus. They prayed long prayers but evicted widows from their homes. They did not care for the poor or the orphans. They sought to convert others, not so they would return to God but so they would be religious like them. It goes on and on.

The religious of today are following the same path as the scribes and Pharisees. Whether they be Christian, Jewish, or Muslim, they make the path back to God complicated and block people who are seeking God from entering into His presence. The Jews deny that Jesus is the Messiah, the Christians stop at the cross, and the Muslims admit Jesus is the Messiah but refuse to see Him as the Son of God.

Eight times in Matthew 23 Jesus tells the religious that woe is upon them for the injustices they commit. This brings to mind Isaiah's response when he found himself standing in God's presence before the throne of God:

> In the year that king Uzziah died I saw also the Lord sitting upon a throne, high and lifted up, and his train filled the temple. Above it stood the seraphims: each one had six wings; with twain he covered his face, and with twain he covered his feet, and with twain he did fly. And one cried unto another, and said, Holy, holy, holy, is the Lord of hosts: the whole earth is full of his glory. And the posts of the door moved at the voice of him that cried, and the house was filled with smoke. Then said I, Woe is me! for I am undone; because I am a man of unclean lips, and I dwell in the midst of a people of unclean lips: for mine eyes have seen the King, the Lord of hosts. Isaiah 6:1-5

When Isaiah found himself face to face with God, he immediately cried out "Woe is me!". Why? Because in the presence of God, neither his sin nor the sin of his people could be denied. In Exodus 33:20, God said to Moses "Thou canst not see my face: for there shall no man see me, and live." Isaiah knew this scripture and was sure he was doomed. Yet God made provision for him, counting Jesus's sacrifice as already accomplished on the altar before His throne and cleansed Isaiah's lips with the burning coal of Jesus sacrifice.

And yet, in the presence of God the Son, the scribes and Pharisees could not recognize their sin. Truly, Isaiah 6:9-10 was still in force when the appointed time for the Messiah came. Religion had blinded the scribes and Pharisees to the prophets, who had described to them the signs of the Messiah so they could recognize Him when He came. Isaiah saw God in the spiritual realm with spiritual eyes, but the religious only saw God in this earthly realm with fleshly eyes.

The principal difference between the Sadducees and Pharisees was that the Sadducees did not believe in resurrection, but, in spite of their differences, both the Sadducees and the Pharisees joined together to test Jesus on numerous occasions, hoping to catch Him in error. Even though Jesus passed each test, they still could not believe in Him as the Messiah. Such is the spirit of religion that puts blinders on the eyes of those who should be able to see and believe but who do not wish to.

So, now we know the bad news is that our relationship with God was broken by man's on-going disobedience and that we cannot restore that relationship ourselves. The serpent continues tempting us to do our own will and to not submit to the will of God.

History shows that mankind's religion cannot restore that relationship and is nothing but a substitute that attempts to manipulate God to submit to man's will.

Perhaps it is time for us to open our spiritual eyes and see that those things we witness in the religious history of the Jewish people are just as real today in the Christian denominations. We, too, have allowed religion to become a substitute for a real relationship with God. We no longer see the signs and wonders following us, which the New Testament promises to those who believe. We do not hear His voice as we should because we do not actually seek a personal relationship with Him. We are led by those who are blind to the truth. We are content with the outward form of religion and choose to believe those signs and wonders promised by Jesus are a thing of the past.

In Revelations 17, we are exposed to a description of religion during the time that the seven vials will be poured out upon the earth.

> And there came one of the seven angels which had the seven vials, and talked with me, saying unto me, Come hither; I will shew unto thee the judgment of the great whore that sitteth upon many waters: With whom the kings of the earth have committed fornication, and the inhabitants of the earth have been made drunk with the wine of her fornication. So he carried me away in the spirit into the wilderness: and I saw a woman sit upon a scarlet coloured beast, full of names of blasphemy, having seven heads and ten horns. And the woman was arrayed in purple and scarlet colour, and decked with gold

and precious stones and pearls, having a golden cup in her hand full of abominations and filthiness of her fornication: And upon her forehead was a name written, MYSTERY, BABYLON THE GREAT, THE MOTHER OF HARLOTS AND ABOMINATIONS OF THE EARTH. And I saw the woman drunken with the blood of the saints, and with the blood of the martyrs of Jesus: and when I saw her, I wondered with great admiration. **Revelation 17:1-6**

In this passage, we see the spirit of religion will play a big part in the plans of the enemy. Comparing Revelations 17:4 and Matthew 23:25, the same description Jesus applied to the scribes and Pharisees applied to this woman so aligned with the beast. She is not the actual city of Babylon but is declared to be a city in Revelations 17:18. Whether she is a physical city or not is a question we must examine. Religion was always the dominate power in cities, even controlling their kings. Whether it was the Temple in Jerusalem, the Vatican in Rome, or the Dome of the Rock in Mecca, religion has exercised its power through the governments of the nations.

The great prostitute is religion in all of its forms. Religion is an outward form of godliness but is inwardly far from God. Religion compromises with the world, seeking after worldly things but failing to seek that restored relationship with God that He desires. Religion seeks its own will rather than God's will. There is hope though. In Revelations 18:4, those who have been able to see the truth are called to come out of religion: "And I heard another voice from heaven, saying, Come out of her, my people, that ye be not partakers of her sins, and that ye receive not of her plagues."

God knows the future. He knows the danger religion holds for His people. A time is coming when He will cry out to His people to come out of religion. Only those who know His voice will hear that cry. Unfortunately, too many will be comfortable in their religion to respond to God's cry.

Just as the Jews waited for their Messiah to come, we wait for His return, thinking it is an event that will happen in some far future we will never see. As we wait, though, it is all too easy to lose the expectation of His eminent return and turn to the world to occupy our time.

The Son of Man

The Messiah has finally come. But who and what is the Messiah? The word "messiah" is מָשִׁיחַ (mâshîyach) in Hebrew and simply means "anointed." Other forms of the word, when used for the anointing of kings or priests in the Old Testament refer to an anointing with oil. Daniel was the only prophet in the Old Testament to refer to the promised opponent of the tempter as the Messiah or Anointed. The passage referring to Christ as the Messiah reads as follows:

> "Know therefore and understand, that from the going forth of the commandment to restore and to build Jerusalem unto the Messiah the Prince shall be seven weeks, and threescore and two weeks: the street shall be built again, and the wall, even in troublous times. And after threescore and two weeks shall Messiah be cut off, but not for himself: and the people of the prince that shall come shall destroy the city and the sanctuary; and the end thereof shall be with a flood, and unto the end of the war desolations are determined" **(Dan. 9:25-26)**.

In John 1:35-41, Andrew shared with his friends that he had found the Messias after overhearing John the Baptist call Jesus "the Lamb of God." The Greek word Μεσσίας or Messias is based on the Hebrew word for

Messiah, Greek being the common language in Israel during the time of Jesus. It is understood that the local dialect of Greek incorporated many Hebrew words much as many Hispanic dialects incorporate local native words.

The first to declare that Jesus was the Son of God was God Himself at Jesus's baptism by John the Baptist (see Matthew 3:17, Mark 1:11, and Luke 3:22). This is also referenced in John 1:15-34 where John bore witness that the Holy Spirit descended upon Jesus. The descent of the Holy Spirit in the form of a dove was the moment of Jesus's anointing as a man by God. The anointing was not done in the traditional manner, with oil poured by a prophet or priest, but with the Holy Spirit by the Father. Anointing symbolizes the assignation of authority and power to act in the name of God and, in the case of Jesus, was done directly by God and not by a prophet sent by God as was done in the Old Testament.

The next person to declare Jesus as the Son of God was Satan during Jesus's temptation in the wilderness (see Matthew 4:1-11 and Luke 4:1-13) followed by the various demons that Jesus cast out (see Matthew 8:29). His identity as the Son of God appears to have been immediately evident to all spiritual beings, perhaps because they all heard God declare Jesus was His Son in the spiritual realms. It was not immediately evident to even His disciples that Jesus was the Son of God. When He walked on water and gave Peter permission to do the same in Matthew 14:22-33, the disciples concluded that Jesus must be the Son of God based on the physical miracle. They needed to rely on the evidence of their own senses since they were deaf to the voice of God, not yet having received the Holy Spirit themselves.

Yet, while Jesus walked in our midst in the flesh, He only referred to Himself as the Son of Man. This is because Jesus was sent with an incredible purpose. He was the only man born of God in the flesh, but His purpose was to be the firstborn of many in the Spirit. He did not walk on this earth as God but as a man who, being without sin, was fully in fellowship and communion with God.

Jesus was not of the generations of fallen men, and therefore the sins of the father mentioned in Exodus 34:7 did not pertain to Him. His Father was God Himself and therefore He was not born with the sin nature all the rest of us inherited from our earthly fathers.

> "And he said unto them, How is it that ye sought me? Wist ye not that I must be about my Father's business?" **(Luke 2:49)**.

Jesus knew His Father from the very beginning. This is seen in His response to His parents when they found Him in the temple as a child in Luke 2:49. His relationship with His Father as a man was developed throughout Jesus's life on this earth. Very early on, He knew what His purpose was here on earth, and He was focused on being fully submitted to His Father's will.

He was the Son of God by His Father, but He was also
the Son of Man through His mother.

Ezekiel was also called "son of man" by God ninety-three
times in the Bible. In Hebrew, בֶּן־אָדָם (pronounced
"ben-'adam") was a term used to denote "mankind"
as a whole. In Hebrew, אִישׁ (pronounced "'îš") denotes
"a man" in the singular tense. Throughout Ezekiel,
God spoke to Ezekiel as if He was speaking to all of
mankind. We may interpret this as Ezekiel being an
intermediary between God and mankind, speaking for
God to the people and representing the people to God.
In this same way, Jesus referring to Himself as the
Son of Man (or as Mankind) illustrates that God had
sent Him to all of mankind to speak as God and, at the
same time, to be mankind's mediator before God.

It is also interesting that Jesus was a man and a
part of mankind but was also God. The passage in
Numbers 23:19 remains true in that Jesus did not lie
nor did He need to repent since He was without sin. A
number of verses declare Jesus as being without sin,
including 1 Peter 2:22 where it says, "Who did no sin,
neither was guile found in his mouth." The Pharisees
did not consider Jesus to be without sin, accusing
Him of blasphemy and of violating the Law of Moses
when He healed a cripple against the rule of working
on the Sabbath. The difference between God's law and
Moses's law was discussed in the previous chapter,
and Jesus was always fully submitted to doing His
Father's will.

There is a more important reason why Jesus always
referred to Himself as the Son of Man. Part of His

mission was to be proof of who we could be if we tried to walk sinless in communion with the Father. In other words, everything Jesus did while He walked in this world, He did as a man, not as God. Every miracle was performed with the power of the Holy Spirit dwelling in Him. He was teaching us how we would be able to walk once we were made sinless through His sacrifice on the cross and received the Holy Spirit as well.

Believe me that I am in the Father, and the Father in me: or else believe me for the very works' sake. Verily, verily, I say unto you, He that believeth on me, the works that I do shall he do also; and greater works than these shall he do; because I go unto my Father. And whatsoever ye shall ask in my name, that will I do, that the Father may be glorified in the Son. **John 14:11-13**

The term "Son of Man" appears eighty-two times in the gospels and it was always by Jesus referring to Himself. In such a way, Jesus constantly stressed His personal identification with mankind.

When Jesus came into the coasts of Caesarea Philippi, he asked his disciples, saying, Whom do men say that I the Son of man am? And they said, Some say that thou art John the Baptist: some, Elias; and others, Jeremias, or one of the prophets. He saith unto them, But whom say ye that I am? And Simon Peter answered and said, Thou art the Christ, the Son of the living God. And Jesus answered and said unto him, Blessed art thou, Simon Barjona: for flesh and blood hath not revealed it unto thee, but my Father which is in heaven. And I say also unto thee, That thou art Peter, and upon this rock I will build

my church; and the gates of hell shall not prevail
against it. And I will give unto thee the keys of the
kingdom of heaven: and whatsoever thou shalt bind
on earth shall be bound in heaven: and whatsoever
thou shalt loose on earth shall be loosed in heaven.
Then charged he his disciples that they should tell no
man that he was Jesus the Christ. **Matthew 16:13-20**

In this passage, Jesus asked His disciples a simple
question: "Who do men think I am?" Of course, men
walk by sight and believe only what they can see or
experience. The carnal man is limited by his five
physical senses in understanding the world around
him. Those senses are inputs to a brain that has been
trained by his culture to interpret the world around
him. The best idea men during His time could have
as to who Jesus was could only be related to what
they had been taught. The closest they could come to
understanding Jesus's purpose was to identify Him as
an incarnation of a prophet from the scriptures or to
confuse Him with John the Baptist, a living prophet.

When Peter declared Jesus was the Christ, the Son of
the living God, Jesus says Peter received a revelation
from the Father. In other words, Peter's declaration was
not based on physical evidence nor on an intellectual
deduction but on personal revelation from the Father.
This personal revelation of Jesus as the Christ is what
the church is founded on. Jesus warned the disciples
not to tell anyone He was the Christ. An intellectual
knowledge of Jesus being the Christ is not enough to
be part of the Body of Christ; it requires a personal
conviction or revelation.

When Jesus submitted to John's baptism, He was exemplifying to mankind the process we must go through to return to God. The first step is repentance, represented by the baptism as detailed in John 1:4 and Acts 19:4.

"John did baptize in the wilderness, and preach the baptism of repentance for the remission of sins" **(Mark 1:4)**.

"Then said Paul, John verily baptized with the baptism of repentance, saying unto the people, that they should believe on him which should come after him, that is, on Christ Jesus" **(Acts 19:4)**.

God sent Jesus to show us the way back to having a real relationship with Him. To do this, Jesus became a teacher and taught first by example. When John the Baptist protested Jesus's submission to baptism, Jesus insisted on it so we would know our need for repentance from sin. Repentance is not a feeling of being sorry for our sin but an action of turning away from our sin. Baptism is an action before witnesses that we choose to no longer walk according to our sin nature but rather to follow a path of righteousness. In many ways, it is a declaration to the world that we will no longer walk in subjection to the ways of the world but are now walking in subjection to the will of God. In other words, we walk not by sight but by faith.

Then cometh Jesus from Galilee to Jordan unto John, to be baptized of him. But John forbad him, saying, I have need to be baptized of thee, and comest thou to me? And Jesus answering said unto him, Suffer it to be so now: for thus it becometh us to fulfil all righteousness. Then he suffered him. And Jesus, when he was baptized, went up straightway out of the water: and, lo, the heavens were opened unto him, and he saw the Spirit of God descending like a dove, and lighting upon him: And lo a voice from heaven, saying, This is my beloved Son, in whom I am well pleased. **Matthew 3:13-17**

By His example, Jesus showed us that true repentance results in an immediate response from God; God's anointing with His Spirit and His declaration of our new relationship with Him is immediate. With His baptism, Jesus began teaching mankind the true path to return to God. Religion teaches us that we have to sacrifice and pay a price for God's favor, but Jesus showed us that we simply need to turn away from ourselves and back to God and He will accept us and bless us. Although this anointing was not immediately available to those baptized by John the Baptist, it became available to all when Jesus completed His work and returned to the Father as promised in John 14:12.

Then Jesus, having received the Holy Spirit, was led by the Holy Spirit into the wilderness to be tempted by Satan. Though it sounds strange to think the Holy Spirit would lead us into those places where we would be tempted, Jesus's actions demonstrate it is so we can learn to overcome the temptation. Jesus's next lesson to us is how to resist the temptation of the world system. As children of the living God, we are no longer of this world system. I repeat, we are to walk by faith, not by sight, despite our sin nature continually calling us back to sin.

As a man, Jesus resisted Satan simply by allowing God to speak through Him. When we are confronted with temptation, we need only to declare God's word with authority. When a Christian declares "It is written!" and speaks God's word, Satan trembles and flees. Why? Because it is God Himself who speaks through us when we are submitted to Him and speak with the authority given to us. We have this authority through Jesus, who was given all authority by God.

The problem in churches today is that most people in the congregation do not study the Word. Reading the Bible, studying it, and memorizing those passages the Holy Spirit shows us are essential to resist temptation. Meditation on the Word allows the Holy Spirit to reveal God's promises to us and our authority to use His word to resist the enemy.

> Submit yourselves therefore to God. Resist the devil, and he will flee from you. Draw nigh to God, and he will draw nigh to you. Cleanse your hands, ye sinners; and purify your hearts, ye double minded. Be afflicted, and mourn, and weep: let your laughter be turned to mourning, and your joy to heaviness. Humble yourselves in the sight of the Lord, and he shall lift you up. **James 4:7-10**

Satan is expert in manipulating our sin nature. As believers, we always will be severely tested by the enemy. Satan wants to see if we are truly submitted to God's will or if we will continue in the same error as Adam, choosing our own will instead. The apostle James was dealing with problems within the church that were the result of a lack of submission to God.

He called the church back to submitting to God and resisting the temptations that were tearing the church apart.

Jesus showed us that walking in this world submitted to God with the Holy Spirit residing within us results in signs and wonders. Healing and other miracles followed Jesus, not because He was the Son of God but because He was the Son of Man without sin submitted to His Father with the power of the Holy Spirit dwelling within. He sent the disciples out two by two to perform the same signs and wonders He did, giving them the authority to do so.

Jesus also showed us the Father's compassion for the poor, widows, and orphans by not treating them as unworthy of God's love. He miraculously fed the multitudes who came to hear Him teach. He forgave those who sinned and called them to repentance. He called Himself the Good Shepherd who sought to feed and protect His flock. He dedicated Himself to His great task and showed us how we also should walk, reflecting God's compassion and forgiveness for us.

Jesus always pointed to God as the Father as He taught about the Kingdom of God. Jesus did not point to Himself. He taught about spiritual things through parables because they help us understand things we cannot perceive with our physical senses. He used illustrations to show us the kingdom of heaven (or of God) because our language is incapable of describing these things. As we develop our spiritual senses, the parables begin to make greater sense to us. Jesus taught that we are able to hear His voice, that we are able see visions and dream dreams, and that we are capable of knowing God's specific will for us.

Jesus walked in our midst, sent by God to speak for God, sharing the Good News, teaching about the kingdom of God and this new relationship as His children, and pastoring those who heard and followed Him. He is the prime example of what modern theologians call the 5-fold ministry; apostle (sent forth), prophet (spokesperson for God), evangelist (bearer of the Good News), pastor (protector of those in His care), and teacher (of the way back to God). We are all to walk the same way, although we may concentrate more in a single aspect of the 5-fold ministry. These are the five principal functions present to edify the body. They were never intended to be titles.

As He lived in our midst, Jesus walked as an example of who we could be if only we were sinless before God. And then, submitted fully to God's will, He went to the cross to pay the ultimate price for our sin so we could be blameless before God. Jesus's work would not be finished until He opened the way for us to return to God.

Rebuilding the Temple

Let us examine the indwelling of the Holy Spirit in us and His role in our spiritual lives. One of the most important relationships we have with God is with the Holy Spirit. In fact, we are referred to in the two letters to the Corinthians as being the Temple of the Holy Spirit. What does this mean?

The Temple in Jerusalem was modeled on the Tabernacle which God commanded Moses to build in Exodus 25-30. In Exodus 25:8, God tells Moses the purpose of the Tabernacle was "that I might dwell among them." The Tabernacle was portable and could move with the Jewish people as they wandered in the wilderness. The Temple in Jerusalem was a permanent structure. The main elements of each were the same.

The Temple was divided in three parts. The outer court was where the people could go to bring their offerings and observe them being sacrificed by the priests. It was in this outer court that Jesus found the merchants and money changers doing business.

> And the Jews' passover was at hand, and Jesus went up to Jerusalem. And found in the temple those that sold oxen and sheep and doves, and the changers of

money sitting: And when he had made a scourge of small cords, he drove them all out of the temple, and the sheep, and the oxen; and poured out the changers' money, and overthrew the tables; And said unto them that sold doves, Take these things hence; make not my Father's house an house of merchandise. And his disciples remembered that it was written, The zeal of thine house hath eaten me up. Then answered the Jews and said unto him, What sign shewest thou unto us, seeing that thou doest these things? Jesus answered and said unto them, Destroy this temple, and in three days I will raise it up. Then said the Jews, Forty and six years was this temple in building, and wilt thou rear it up in three days? But he spake of the temple of his body. When therefore he was risen from the dead, his disciples remembered that he had said this unto them; and they believed the scripture, and the word which Jesus had said. **John 2:13-22**

Why was this a problem for Jesus? Because, instead of the people bringing a sacrifice to the Temple out of the best of their own possessions, the people were being allowed to purchase a substitute offering. In other words, it was no longer a real sacrificial giving on the part of the people but a convenience to comply with religious tradition. These were not offerings that were pleasing to God.

We can see how important the sanctity of the Temple was to Jesus. The way the Temple was being misused was indicative of the fallen nature of Jewish society and of their religious nature, especially that of the priests and religious leaders who permitted these money changers to do business in the Temple. The

Temple was not being served by the priests and used to strengthen the people's faith but was being used instead for their own profit. The Messiah saw that corruption had reached the highest levels of the priestly hierarchy and that the people had transferred their faith from God to religion.

It is important to note in this passage that it was not the scribes and Pharisees who asked Jesus for a sign. It was the people who were selling sacrificial animals and changing money. They had heard of Jesus and that signs and wonders followed Him. Perhaps they wanted to see a show by this holy man. Or possibly, they wanted Him to fail in producing these signs and wonders so they could justify continuing what they were doing. The answer He gave them was not what they were expecting. When He answered them in John 2:19, they thought He was referring to rebuilding the Temple in only three days, which would clearly have been impossible. It wasn't until later the disciples realized Jesus was speaking of His body being the Temple. Paul explains in 2 Corinthians 6:13-18 what Jesus meant by that. You can see a direct correlation between the passage in John and the passage in 2 Corinthians.

> Be ye not unequally yoked together with unbelievers: for what fellowship hath righteousness with unrighteousness? and what communion hath light with darkness? And what concord hath Christ with Belial? or what part hath he that believeth with an infidel? And what agreement hath the temple of God with idols? for ye are the temple of the living God; as God hath said, I will dwell in them, and walk in *them*;

and I will be their God, and they shall be my people. Wherefore come out from among them, and be ye separate, saith the Lord, and touch not the unclean *thing*; and I will receive you, And will be a Father unto you, and ye shall be my sons and daughters, saith the Lord Almighty. **2 Corinthians 6:14-18**

The money changers and those who sold animals for sacrifice in the Temple in John's passage are referred to as the unbelievers in 2 Corinthians 6:14. Those who are religious for profit are unbelievers. Not every religious unbeliever makes money from their religious attitudes, but they all expect to benefit in some way from their religious practices. They try to manipulate God or gain favor with God by fasting or by their works. But their religious practices are shown to be the same as idols in 2 Corinthians 6:16.

We are declared to be temples of the Living God just as Jesus referred to Himself as a temple. The church is the Body of Christ, but each believer in the church is a temple of the Holy Spirit as explained in 1 Corinthians 3:16. The Holy Spirit has taken up residence in us. Just as Jesus perceived the money changers in the outer court of the Temple, the religious have reasoned ways to profit from their "faith". We are warned against defiling the Temple, but this does not refer to our sin, which was taken care of on the cross, but rather by our carnal attitude of religion. We wish to be seen as good Christians and act holy when others see us. We look for approval from the church instead of from God. We hope to gain a good reputation for our own profit. This is the wisdom of this world.

Know ye not that ye are the temple of God, and that the Spirit of God dwelleth in you? If any man defile the temple of God, him shall God destroy; for the temple of God is holy, which temple ye are. Let no man deceive himself. If any man among you seemeth to be wise in this world, let him become a fool, that he may be wise. For the wisdom of this world is foolishness with God. For it is written, He taketh the wise in their own craftiness. And again, The Lord knoweth the thoughts of the wise, that they are vain. Therefore let no man glory in men. For all things are your's; Whether Paul, or Apollos, or Cephas, or the world, or life, or death, or things present, or things to come; all are your's; And ye are Christ's; and Christ is God's. **1 Corinthians 3:16-23**

This passage is usually interpreted as the temple of God being our physical bodies and that sinning, especially sins of the flesh, defiles the temple in a physical sense. However, the Bible clearly states we are a tri-part being consisting of body, soul, and spirit (see 1 Thessalonians 5:23). Our body or flesh inhabits and interprets the world around us, and our mind interacts with the flesh and with the spirit. Our spirit connects us to God and allows our mind or self to know God.

Ye worship ye know not what: we know what we worship: for salvation is of the Jews. But the hour cometh, and now is, when the true worshippers shall worship the Father in spirit and in truth: for the Father seeketh such to worship him. God is a Spirit: and they that worship him must worship him in spirit and in truth. **John 4:22-24**

As I meditated on these verses, I came to realize the layout of the Temple, or Tabernacle, mirrors the tripart nature of man. The outer court represents the outer man which interacts with the physical world. The Holy Place represents the soul or mind of man. The Holy of Holies represents the spirit of man, that part of man which is God-breathed and capable of communicating with God. Without Jesus, the natural man only knows the first two parts of the tabernacle because the veil of his sin nature does not allow him access to the Holy of Holies. Once we receive the Holy Spirit, the Holy of Holies within us is where the presence of God dwells. The reality is that His Spirit dwells in our spirit, not in our flesh.

The Holy Place in the temple contains the Altar of Incense, the Menorah, and the Table of Showbread. Our soul is able to offer incense (praise) either to God or to our flesh. Likewise, our soul can offer the light or life we possess to God or to our flesh, and our soul can offer our sacrifices (Showbread) to God or to our flesh. The direction of our praise, life, and sacrifice depends on if we submit our free will to God or to our flesh.

The Holy Spirit does not directly move our flesh. The Spirit reveals God's will, and if our spirit is submitted to the Holy Spirit, our spirit will direct our flesh via our soul to accomplish God's purpose. The Spirit cannot direct those who are not submitted to God because God gave us all free will. A true follower of Christ will submit his free will to obey the direction of the Holy Spirit.

Free will is a characteristic of the soul and is exercised by the soul to direct the flesh. Our free will manifests as our sin nature when it is not submitted to God. But likewise, it will manifest as our divine nature when we are submitted to God within us, the Holy Spirit.

Our flesh is only a temporary housing for our soul and spirit. Our bodies will return to the dust from which they were made. However, God's temple in us is meant to endure forever, just as His Spirit dwells in us forever.

The religious leaders in the time of Christ ridiculed Him for declaring that He would rebuild the Temple in three days. But He was the temple of the Holy Spirit while He walked this earth. In their persecution, the Jews tore down the true Temple (Christ) and, three days after His crucifixion, He rose again and finished His work in the disciples who followed Him. He gave them the Great Commission, and when He returned to the Father, He sent the Holy Spirit to dwell within their spirits, giving them the same power He exercised while He walked among them. Now there are many temples but one God, many spirits but one Holy Spirit.

Tearing Down Walls

As Jesus walked in the midst of Israel, He began fulfilling all of the prophesies spoken of concerning the Messiah in the Old Testament. However, the manner in which He fulfilled the prophesies did not align with the expectations of the various religious sects and caused a great deal of conflict with the religious beliefs of the day. That is because the messianic prophesies in the Old Testament are concerned with the spiritual purposes of God through Jesus and not with the political and religious expectations of Israel. Even the disciples were confused as to what Jesus was doing.

The Pharisees and Sadducees attempted numerous times to discredit Jesus, asking Him questions concerning their own doctrines in the hopes of catching Him saying something in conflict with their view of the law. For the Jewish religious sects, Jesus was a very real threat. He was systematically challenging their religious beliefs and dismantling their religious paradigms through His teachings and miracles. Jesus was ripping away the veil of religion that was hiding God from His people. Jesus's miracles were seen by the masses as evidence that what He was teaching was divine truth, though the religious only saw their belief system being challenged.

The Jewish religion in biblical times was based on strict adherence to Mosaic Law. Not all of Mosaic Law was given by God. (I question whether or not the Jewish nation then elevated Moses to be equal to God concerning disobedience to God's commandment of not having any other gods before Him.) God's law is characterized by love. Over millennia, the Law of Moses was expounded upon by religious theologians applying intellect and logic to interpret and expand upon the law until, as Jesus stated in Luke 11:46, it became a grievous burden to the people of Israel. Jesus instead simplified the entirety of the law to just two commandments:

> Hearing that Jesus had silenced the Sadducees, the Pharisees got together. One of them, an expert in the law, tested him with this question: "Teacher, which is the greatest commandment in the Law?" Jesus replied: "'Love the Lord your God with all your heart and with all your soul and with all your mind.' This is the first and greatest commandment. And the second is like it: 'Love your neighbor as yourself.' All the Law and the Prophets hang on these two commandments." **Matthew 22:34-40**

If we apply this declaration by Jesus to all of the laws of Moses, few of them would pass the love test. In other words, most of Mosaic law was given for the purposes of governing the nation. Considering that Moses was raised as Egyptian royalty, I wonder how much of Mosaic Law was founded on Egyptian law, how much on traditions of the nation of Israel, and how much on revelation from God. I do not have the expertise to evaluate such a speculation and must make sure the reader understands this statement is purely speculation.

The religious leaders of Jesus's time took great pride in their literal adherence to the Law of Moses, yet they did not seem to have a clue as to what it meant to abide by the spirit of the law. They took pride in presenting an outward adherence to the law but did not let the spirit of the law govern their hearts. Their religious dogma incorporated religious traditions that had little or nothing to do with God's law nor the Law of Moses.

In Matthew 23, Jesus declared seven woes upon the scribes and Pharisees. As I meditated on this, I came to realize Jesus was literally tearing down religious practices that had kept the people of God bound and unable to return to God. Let us look at these seven woes or judgements.

> Then spake Jesus to the multitude, and to his disciples, Saying The scribes and the Pharisees sit in Moses' seat: All therefore whatsoever they bid you observe, that observe and do; but do not ye after their works: for they say, and do not. For they bind heavy burdens and grievous to be borne, and lay them on men's shoulders; but they themselves will not move them with one of their fingers. But all their works they do for to be seen of men: they make broad their phylacteries, and enlarge the borders of their garments, And love the uppermost rooms at feasts,

and the chief seats in the synagogues, And greetings in the markets, and to be called of men, Rabbi, Rabbi. But be not ye called Rabbi: for one is your Master, even Christ; and all ye are brethren. And call no man your father upon the earth: for one is your Father, which is in heaven. Neither be ye called masters: for one is your Master, even Christ. But he that is greatest among you shall be your servant. And whosoever shall exalt himself shall be abased; and he that shall humble himself shall be exalted. **Matthew 23:1-12**

Jesus identified clearly that He was speaking to the scribes, who were the theologians in Jesus's time, and to the Pharisees, who were thes most powerful of the religious sects. Although He commanded the people of Israel to observe what they taught, He warned them not to do what they did, with the attitudes that they had.

Jesus called the scribes and Pharisees out about how they had made the Law so burdensome that no one could enter God's presence, including themselves. In Matthew 23:13-14 , He says, "But woe unto you, scribes and Pharisees, hypocrites! for ye shut up the kingdom of heaven against men: for ye neither go in yourselves, neither suffer ye them that are entering to go in. Woe unto you, scribes and Pharisees, hypocrites! for ye devour widows' houses, and for a pretence make long prayer: therefore ye shall receive the greater damnation."

Jesus also showed their motivations were not holy. They showed their piety in public and their greed in private. They were two-faced and had no real integrity. As followers of Christ, we are called to live lives of integrity, being the same in private as we are in public.

Next, Jesus showed how these groups went to great lengths to add followers to their sects, teaching them to be just like they were. They did not call people to God but to themselves. Instead of seeking God themselves, they sought followers.

> Woe unto you, scribes and Pharisees, hypocrites! for ye compass sea and land to make one proselyte, and when he is made, ye make him twofold more the child of hell than yourselves. Woe unto you, ye blind guides, which say, Whosoever shall swear by the temple, it is nothing; but whosoever shall swear by the gold of the temple, he is a debtor! Ye fools and blind: for whether is greater, the gold, or the temple that sanctifieth the gold? And, Whosoever shall swear by the altar, it is nothing; but whosoever sweareth by the gift that is upon it, he is guilty. Ye fools and blind: for whether is greater, the gift, or the altar that sanctifieth the gift? Whoso therefore shall swear by the altar, sweareth by it, and by all things thereon. And whoso shall swear by the temple, sweareth by it, and by him that dwelleth therein. And he that shall swear by heaven, sweareth by the throne of God, and by him that sitteth thereon. **Matthew 23:15-22**

Be aware these verses apply to all who make oaths, not only to the religious. Be careful who or what you are making your oaths to and whose advice you follow when making an oath.

The fourth judgement concerns following the letter of the law without considering the spirit of the law. Jesus said in Matthew 23:23-24: "Woe unto you, scribes and Pharisees, hypocrites! for ye pay tithe of mint and anise and cumin, and have omitted the weightier matters of the law, judgment, mercy, and faith: these ought ye to have done, and not to leave the other undone. Ye blind guides, which strain at a gnat, and swallow a camel." Jesus considered the spirit of the law was to express the love of God through judgment, mercy and faith. In love, all the law is fulfilled.

> Woe unto you, scribes and Pharisees, hypocrites! for ye make clean the outside of the cup and of the platter, but within they are full of extortion and excess. Thou blind Pharisee, cleanse first that which is within the cup and platter, that the outside of them may be clean also. Woe unto you, scribes and Pharisees, hypocrites! for ye are like unto whited sepulchres, which indeed appear beautiful outward, but are within full of dead men's bones, and of all uncleanness. Even so ye also outwardly appear righteous unto men, but within ye are full of hypocrisy and iniquity. **Matthew 23:25-28**

Jesus addressed outward appearances versus inner reality with his words above. The religious tried to convince their followers that what they displayed in public was indicative of their inner reality despite their inward reality being diametrically opposed to their outer appearance. Jesus pronounced woe upon them because they presented an appearance of having spiritual life, while in fact they were spiritually dead. This false path led many to continue a spiritual walk of death instead of seeking the narrow door that opens onto the path of spiritual life.

In Matthew 23:29-39, Jesus delivered His next criticism. He shows how the religious condemn the righteous, in this case, the prophets. After judging the prophets and killing them, they then honor them, while saying that they would never do what their forefathers had done in killing the prophets.

Woe unto you, scribes and Pharisees, hypocrites! because ye build the tombs of the prophets, and garnish the sepulchres of the righteous, And say, If we had been in the days of our fathers, we would not have been partakers with them in the blood of the prophets. Wherefore ye be witnesses unto yourselves, that ye are the children of them which killed the prophets. Fill ye up then the measure of your fathers. Ye serpents, ye generation of vipers, how can ye escape the damnation of hell? Wherefore, behold, I send unto you prophets, and wise men, and scribes: and some of them ye shall kill and crucify; and some of them shall ye scourge in your synagogues, and persecute them from city to city: That upon you may come all the righteous blood shed upon the earth, from the blood of righteous Abel unto the blood of Zacharias son of Barachias, whom ye slew between the temple and the altar. Verily I say unto you, All these things shall come upon this generation. O Jerusalem, Jerusalem, thou that killest the prophets, and stonest them which are sent unto thee, how often would I have gathered thy children together, even as a hen gathereth her chickens under her wings, and ye would not! Behold, your house is left unto you desolate. For I say unto you, Ye shall not see me henceforth, till ye shall say, Blessed is he that cometh in the name of the Lord.
Matthew 23:29-39

Matthew 23 is a long passage, but it expresses Jesus's contempt for the religious sects of His day. Jesus revealed to the religious leaders that woe would come upon them for what they had done to God's word and to God's people. Seven times, Jesus circled the walls of religion, much like the Jewish nation did around the city of Jericho to bring down its walls, but He would give a great shout from the cross and those walls of religion would come tumbling down.

In response to Jesus's observations, those prominent religious leaders then prepared false witnesses against Him. They accused Him of blasphemy in violation of the law against bearing false witness, citing Exodus 20:16. Hypocrisy indeed!

In the beginning of Matthew 26, Jesus predicted His own crucifixion.

> And it came to pass, when Jesus had finished all these sayings, he said unto his disciples, Ye know that after two days is the feast of the passover, and the Son of man is betrayed to be crucified. Then assembled together the chief priests, and the scribes, and the elders of the people, unto the palace of the high priest, who was called Caiaphas, And consulted that they might take Jesus by subtilty, and kill him. But they said, Not on the feast day, lest there be an uproar among the people. **Matthew 26: 1-5**

Jesus knew beforehand what manner of sacrifice He would be required to pay to fulfill His Father's will. He knew the Sanhedrim would act to silence Him. When He went to the Garden of Gethsemane to pray, He cried out to the Father to let this cup pass from Him but still submitted to His Father's will. (see Matthew 26:36-46) He resisted the greatest temptation of all; to save His life by turning away from doing His Fathers will.

The Cross and the Veil

It is likely most people reading this book are already familiar with the circumstances and events leading up to Jesus's crucifixion as the crucifixion story is central to the Christian faith. Without going into a great deal of detail regarding the crucifixion, there are a few things the Holy Spirit has shown me about this key point in mankind's history that may not have been explored by most of us.

Jesus knew beforehand every aspect of what was to happen to Him. He knew exactly where He would keep the Passover (see Matthew 26:18). He knew one of the disciples would betray Him and He knew exactly which one it would be. He knew exactly what manner of sacrifice He would be required to make.

> And as they did eat, he said, Verily I say unto you, that one of you shall betray me. And they were exceeding sorrowful, and began every one of them to say unto him, Lord, is it I? And he answered and said, He that dippeth his hand with me in the dish, the same shall betray me. The Son of man goeth as it is written of him: but woe unto that man by whom the Son of man is betrayed! it had been good for that man if he had not been born. Then Judas, which betrayed him, answered and said, Master, is it I? He said unto him, Thou hast said. **Matthew 26:21-25**

Jesus possessed the spiritual gift of the word of knowledge. Some might say He was prophesying His death. Prophecy is not about seeing the future but about warning of the consequences if we do not change from the path we are on. A prophet is a watchman who sees danger approaching and calls out a warning. We see this in the book of the prophet Ezekiel when he was called to be a prophet as well as in the books of many of the other prophets.

> "Son of man, I have made thee a watchman unto the house of Israel: therefore hear the word at my mouth, and give them warning from me" **(Ezek. 3:17)**.

> "So thou, O son of man, I have set thee a watchman unto the house of Israel; therefore thou shalt hear the word at my mouth, and warn them from me" **(Ezek. 33:1-7)**.

The word of knowledge is a spiritual gift that reveals knowledge of things we have no way of knowing in the natural. The word of knowledge is knowledge revealed by God, who is omnipotent, through the Holy Spirit for a purpose. Though Jesus would be tempted to turn away from what the Father called Him to do, foreknowing what was ahead strengthened His resolve.

> And we know that all things work together for good to them that love God, to them who are the called according to his purpose. For whom he did foreknow, he also did predestinate to be conformed to the image of his Son, that he might be the firstborn among many brethren. Moreover whom he did predestinate, them he also called: and whom he called, them he also justified: and whom he justified, them he also glorified. **Romans 8:28-30**

Even though the Sanhedrin did not have the legal power to crucify Jesus under Roman law, Jesus knew He would be crucified by these religious leaders for what He taught. He knew all the remaining prophecies concerning Him would be fulfilled before He died on the cross, including the prophecy found in Isaiah 53.

Who hath believed our report? and to whom is the arm of the Lord revealed? For he shall grow up before him as a tender plant, and as a root out of a dry ground: he hath no form nor comeliness; and when we shall see him, there is no beauty that we should desire him. He is despised and rejected of men; a man of sorrows, and acquainted with grief: and we hid as it were our faces from him; he was despised, and we esteemed him not. Surely he hath borne our griefs, and carried our sorrows: yet we did esteem him stricken, smitten of God, and afflicted. But he was wounded for our transgressions, he was bruised for our iniquities: the chastisement of our peace was upon him; and with his stripes we are healed. All we like sheep have gone astray; we have turned every one to his own way; and the Lord hath laid on him the iniquity of us all. He was oppressed, and he was afflicted, yet he opened not his mouth: he is brought as a lamb to the slaughter, and as a sheep before her shearers is dumb, so he openeth not his mouth. He was taken from prison and from judgment: and who shall declare his generation? for he was cut off out of the land of the living: for the transgression of my people was he stricken. And he made his grave with the wicked, and with the rich in his death; because he had done no violence, neither was any deceit in his mouth. Yet it pleased the Lord to bruise him; he hath put him to grief: when thou shalt make his soul an offering for sin, he shall see his seed, he shall prolong his days, and the pleasure of the Lord shall prosper in his hand. He shall see of the travail of his soul, and shall be satisfied: by his knowledge shall my righteous servant justify many; for he shall bear their iniquities. Therefore will I divide him a portion with the great, and he shall divide the spoil with the strong; because he hath poured out his soul unto death: and he was numbered with the transgressors; and he bare the sin of many, and made intercession for the transgressors. **Isaiah 53:1-12**

In the garden of Gethsemane, Jesus warned His disciples about the temptations they would face in the coming weeks. We often think only of the temptations common to man as the ones we need to resist, but Jesus showed the disciples three very important temptations they needed to guard against.

The first temptation He cautioned them about is the temptation to sleep instead of being watchful. Jesus asked the disciples in Matthew 26:41 to watch and pray as He prepared himself on the mountain. Why? In order that they would understand the events soon to occur were necessary and to not react in the manner they did. Jesus had already outlined all that would occur to Him, the judgement of men, the scourging, and the events culminating with His death on the cross, but still, they did not keep watch. In Matthew 26:31, He specifically told them that these things would occur that very night. But they slumbered instead of being vigilant, and they misunderstood what was happening when Judas came and kissed Jesus, the telling signal to those who had come to take Him. We also, as followers of Christ, need to maintain spiritual vigilance and not allow ourselves to be distracted by the concerns of the world around us. Taking our spiritual eyes off of Jesus allows the world system the opportunity to sing us a "lullaby" to put our spirit to sleep.

The second temptation is to react in the flesh instead of in the Spirit. Matthew, Mark, and Luke all record that "one of them" drew his sword and struck a servant of the high priest, cutting off his ear. John specifically named Peter as the one who did this. Immediately after this act, Jesus reprimanded the disciples for reacting with violence. This is always going to be our go-to when threatened. When we walk according to the flesh, our natural response is to fight or flee. In the spirit, we need to let God guide our responses.

> Then said Jesus unto him, Put up again thy sword into his place: for all they that take the sword shall perish with the sword. Thinkest thou that I cannot now pray to my Father, and he shall presently give me more than twelve legions of angels? But how then shall the scriptures be fulfilled, that thus it must be? **Matthew 26:52-54**

After walking with Jesus all this time, the disciples should have understood each of the events leading to the cross had to occur to fulfill scripture. Jesus still had lessons to teach them, ones He continues to teach us to this day.

The third temptation concerns self-defense. Jesus showed by His example that we must submit to God's will even if it means there is a possibility of our going through excruciating pain and death to obey. Yet, even after Jesus warned him that he would deny Jesus three times in order to hide from those who would judge him, Peter still denied Jesus three times. Fear can make us forget all we have been warned against in its demand for us to fight or flee. We all desire to defend ourselves. Whether it is our lives that are threatened, our reputation, or our own self-image; we want to protect ourselves. But we should not react the way Adam and Eve did, which was in the flesh. We must trust God and rely on His protection as we submit to Him and obey.

As followers of Christ, we must resist temptation in all its forms. We may fail often, but we can repent, ask forgiveness, and move forward. The three temptations we must be the most on guard against are lacking vigilance, reacting in the flesh, and fearing for ourselves. We are not of this world and must learn to walk a different way, following Jesus by His example into the presence of the Father.

Jesus was betrayed, but He was not surprised by it. He was judged by the Sanhedrin, including by the high priest, Caiaphas. The scribes and elders brought false witnesses against Him, but Jesus held His peace. He was brought to the Roman governor, Pontius Pilate, for judgement according to Roman law and still did not defend Himself. The Roman governor found Him blameless, but these religious leaders insisted that He be crucified for His blasphemy.

I find it interesting that Pontius Pilate washed his hands and declared that he would not be responsible for the blood of an innocent man. All the people who were present cried out "His blood be on us, and on our children" (Matt. 27:25). In truth, His blood was shed for all of us; He washed away our sins with His blood so it is indeed on us and on our children. When Jesus finally cried out "It is finished" (John 19:30), He paid the price even for those who crucified Him, parted His clothes, and pierced His side.

> Jesus, when he had cried again with a loud voice, yielded up the ghost. And, behold, the veil of the temple was rent in twain from the top to the bottom; and the earth did quake, and the rocks rent; And the graves were opened; and many bodies of the saints which slept arose, And came out of the graves after his resurrection, and went into the holy city, and appeared unto many. **Matthew 27:50-53**

Jesus finished the work the Father gave Him, paying the price for our sins, when He died on the cross. Yet the scripture above portends the next important event was His burial and resurrection. I think, however, a more important event was God's sign that Jesus's sacrifice was accepted. Jesus's sacrifice won our access to the Holy of Holies and the very presence of the Living God. The barrier that kept mankind from having a relationship with God was now breached; our sin nature as represented by the veil was no longer a barrier to a relationship with God.

The veil in the Temple hid God from His people. Aside from the artistry that went into it, its purpose was to

separate men from God's presence. It was not there
to protect God from man. Only the High Priest, after
a ritual of sanctification, was allowed to enter once
a year to offer the blood and incense sacrifices for
the sins of the people. The understanding was that if
sinful man came into the presence of God, or saw God,
he would perish. When Isaiah found himself in the
throne room of God, he cried out in despair because
his eyes had seen God.

> In the year that king Uzziah died I saw also the LORD
> sitting upon a throne, high and lifted up, and his
> train filled the temple. Above it stood the seraphims:
> each one had six wings; with twain he covered his
> face, and with twain he covered his feet, and with
> twain he did fly. And one cried unto another, and
> said, Holy, holy, holy, is the LORD of hosts: the whole
> earth is full of his glory. And the posts of the door
> moved at the voice of him that cried, and the house
> was filled with smoke. Then said I, Woe is me! for I
> am undone; because I am a man of unclean lips, and
> I dwell in the midst of a people of unclean lips: for
> mine eyes have seen the King, the LORD of hosts.
> **Isaiah 6:1-5**

Therefore, the veil can be viewed as representing
all things that keep us from fellowship with God, a
fellowship Adam and Eve enjoyed, which was broken
by their rebellion in the Garden of Eden. These things
include our sin, weakness, fear, doubt, rebellion, and
so on, which we cannot overcome on our own.

The sacrifices offered by the High Priest only covered
the sins of the past year. Our sin nature immediately
tempts us to sin after each offering, so we are never

able to have true fellowship with God. That sounds like an impossible situation for us, but by Jesus's sacrifice, the impossible is made possible. This is explained in Hebrews 10:1-4.

> For the law having a shadow of good things to come, and not the very image of the things, can never with those sacrifices which they offered year by year continually make the comers thereunto perfect. For then would they not have ceased to be offered? because that the worshippers once purged should have had no more conscience of sins. But in those sacrifices there is a remembrance again made of sins every year. For it is not possible that the blood of bulls and of goats should take away sins.

The book of Hebrews also says Jesus, being the new and living way, expects us to enter into the presence of the Living God through the veil, which He opened for us by the sacrifice of His flesh. When His flesh died, the veil was torn from the top down.

> Having therefore, brethren, boldness to enter into the holiest by the blood of Jesus, By a new and living way, which he hath consecrated for us, through the veil, that is to say, his flesh; And having an high priest over the house of God; Let us draw near with a true heart in full assurance of faith, having our hearts sprinkled from an evil conscience, and our bodies washed with pure water. Let us hold fast the profession of our faith without wavering; (for he is faithful that promised;) **Hebrews 10:19-23**

Note that the veil was not cast down but that a way was made through it. Our sin nature (the veil) remains, but our sin has been dealt with. We can now survive being in the presence of God as our past, present, and future sin has been forgiven.

There are two other passages where Jesus Himself spoke about following Him.

> Jesus saith unto him, I am the way, the truth, and the life: no man cometh unto the Father, but by me. If ye had known me, ye should have known my Father also: and from henceforth ye know him, and have seen him. Philip saith unto him, Lord, show us the Father, and it sufficeth us. Jesus saith unto him, Have I been so long time with you, and yet hast thou not known me, Philip? he that hath seen me hath seen the Father; and how sayest thou then, Show us the Father? Believest thou not that I am in the Father, and the Father in me? the words that I speak unto you I speak not of myself: but the Father that dwelleth in me, he doeth the works. Believe me that I am in the Father, and the Father in me: or else believe me for the very works' sake. **John 14:6-11**

Saying, The Son of man must suffer many things, and be rejected of the elders and chief priests and scribes, and be slain, and be raised the third day. And he said to them all, If any man will come after me, let him deny himself, and take up his cross daily, and follow me. For whosoever will save his life shall lose it: but whosoever will lose his life for my sake, the same shall save it. For what is a man advantaged, if he gain the whole world, and lose himself, or be cast away? For whosoever shall be ashamed of me and of my words, of him shall the Son of man be ashamed, when he shall come in his own glory, and in his Father's, and of the holy angels. But I tell you of a truth, there be some standing here, which shall not taste of death, till they see the kingdom of God. **Luke 19:22-27**

It is very clear from these passages that Jesus expected those who believed in Him to follow Him through the veil and into the presence of God. He also explained the purpose of His crucifixion was to open the way to enter into a relationship with God.

Jesus used the gender-based term "Father" to denote the closest familial relationship God wants to have with us. God wants a close personal relationship with each of us as individuals. He does not see us as male or female but as His children. (It truly is difficult not to use pronouns when referring to God!) The term Father denotes a familial relationship, one exercising familial authority, yet also describing a close, loving relationship. There are other societies that are not patriarchies which may use a different familial relationship to describe this. The gender of the term is not important but the relationship is.

A relationship does not start full blown but develops over time. A newborn child learns who his parents are by hearing their voices and seeing their actions as they provide care and by the interactive responses between them over time. He comes to trust them, to recognize their voices and faces, and, eventually, to understand their words. We, as God's children, need to follow the same process in developing a relationship with Him; trusting, hearing, and obeying.

This is why Jesus went to the cross. It was not to give us a "Get Out of Hell Free" card but to open the way for us to know God and to form a close, loving relationship with Him. When Jesus went to the Father, He sent the Holy Spirit to dwell within us.

> Nevertheless I tell you the truth; It is expedient for you that I go away: for if I go not away, the Comforter will not come unto you; but if I depart, I will send him unto you. And when he is come, he will reprove the world of sin, and of righteousness, and of judgment: Of sin, because they believe not on me; Of righteousness, because I go to my Father, and ye see me no more; Of judgment, because the prince of this world is judged. I have yet many things to say unto you, but ye cannot bear them now. Howbeit when he, the Spirit of truth, is come, he will guide you into all truth: for he shall not speak of himself; but whatsoever he shall hear, that shall he speak: and he will shew you things to come. He shall glorify me: for he shall receive of mine, and shall shew it unto you.
> **John 16:7-14**

The Spirit was sent to convince us of our sin (not convict as in a court of law) and to lead us into all truth. Only one sin remains for the Spirit to convince us of. The unforgivable sin is not believing in Jesus and not believing He was sent of the Father to pay the price for our sin. It is not believing that Jesus, as the Son of Man, showed us by His words and actions that we can do everything He did while walking in the flesh. It is not seeing that Jesus sent us the Holy Spirit to give us the power to walk as He walked and to teach us how to live in the spirit and not in the flesh.

"Verily, verily, I say unto you, He that believeth on me, the works that I do shall he do also; and greater works than these shall he do; because I go unto my Father" **(John 14:12)**.

As I reflect on my walk with Jesus, I see the Holy Spirit took the doctrines of man religion taught and revealed they were a very superficial, intellectual understanding of the Word. The doctrines that were the milk that Paul spoke about in Hebrews 5:13-14 were similarly an intellectual understanding: "For every one that useth milk is unskilful in the word of righteousness: for he is a babe. But strong meat belongeth to them that are of full age, even those who by reason of use have their senses exercised to discern both good and evil." (Heb. 5:13-14). The people could not receive strong spiritual meat until their spiritual senses had been exercised. They could not be led of the Spirit if they could not hear His voice and see the path before them.

> Then came the Jews round about him, and said unto him, How long dost thou make us to doubt? If thou be the Christ, tell us plainly. Jesus answered them, I told you, and ye believed not: the works that I do in my Father's name, they bear witness of me. But ye believe not, because ye are not of my sheep, as I said unto you. My sheep hear my voice, and I know them, and they follow me: And I give unto them eternal life; and they shall never perish, neither shall any man pluck them out of my hand. My Father, which gave them me, is greater than all; and no man is able to pluck them out of my Father's hand. I and my Father are one. **John 10:24-30**

I have learned I cannot impart revelation to anyone. Likewise, Paul could not impart revelation either. He could only teach what his disciples could understand intellectually. Only the Spirit can reveal those spiritual things Paul refers to as strong meat. Paul strove to encourage his disciples to seek after the knowledge of God, learning to exercise their spiritual senses so they could hear Him and follow Him. He instructs of this in Romans 10:17: "So then faith cometh by hearing, and hearing by the word of God."

Please note that the word of God here in Romans refers to *rhema*, the utterance of God, and not to *logos*, the written Word of God. Faith comes by spiritually hearing God speak to you. When you can clearly recognize when God is speaking directly to you, faith is made easy.

The Holy Spirit wants to reveal the deep currents of the Spirit to those who diligently seek Him. This is the reward spoken of in Hebrews 11:6: "But without faith *it is* impossible to please *him*: for he that cometh to God must believe that he is, and *that* he is a rewarder of them that diligently seek him."

> That the God of our Lord Jesus Christ, the Father of glory, may give unto you the spirit of wisdom and revelation in the knowledge of him: The eyes of your understanding being enlightened; that ye may know what is the hope of his calling, and what the riches of the glory of his inheritance in the saints, And what is the exceeding greatness of his power to us-ward who believe, according to the working of his mighty power. **Ephesians 1:17-19**

The Holy Spirit is the revealer of the deep things of God, but He cannot reveal those things to those who are deaf, dumb, and blind spiritually. He is the Spirit of Revelation and Wisdom and wants to move us into the deep waters of our spiritual nature. Only then can we truly experience what it is to be His body.

Followers of Christ

What does it really mean to be a Christian? Does it mean your parents had you baptized as a child or that you were raised in a home that had a Bible on the coffee table? Does it mean you believe in the historical figure of Christ even though you do not know much about Him? Does it mean everything you know about Jesus is from the stories on TV during Christmas and Easter and you believe those things did happen? Perhaps you were raised in a church and attend regularly, and even go to prayer meetings and Bible studies. But does any of this really mean you are a Christian in the biblical sense?

Let's examine what Scripture says about the first Christians:

> When they heard these things, they held their peace, and glorified God, saying, Then hath God also to the Gentiles granted repentance unto life. Now they which were scattered abroad upon the persecution that arose about Stephen travelled as far as Phenice, and Cyprus, and Antioch, preaching the word to none but unto the Jews only. And some of them were men of Cyprus and Cyrene, which, when they were come to Antioch, spake unto the Grecians, preaching the Lord Jesus. And the hand of the Lord was with

107

them: and a great number believed, and turned unto the Lord. Then tidings of these things came unto the ears of the church which was in Jerusalem: and they sent forth Barnabas, that he should go as far as Antioch. Who, when he came, and had seen the grace of God, was glad, and exhorted them all, that with purpose of heart they would cleave unto the Lord. For he was a good man, and full of the Holy Ghost and of faith: and much people was added unto the Lord. Then departed Barnabas to Tarsus, for to seek Saul: And when he had found him, he brought him unto Antioch. And it came to pass, that a whole year they assembled themselves with the church, and taught much people. And the disciples were called Christians first in Antioch. **Acts 11:18-26**

In this passage from the book of Acts, disciples or students of Christ were called Christians. In this particular case, they were Gentiles who believed the message of Christ and were being discipled by the apostles. The apostles were the teachers in this context, but they also were disciples of Jesus, not only while He walked with them on earth but also through the guidance of the Holy Spirit. Jesus Christ sent them forth into the world with the Holy Spirit, giving them the power to forgive people's sins, thereby giving witness to the Good News (see John 20:21-23).

When Jesus walked with them, the disciples followed Jesus wherever He went, learning from their Master by His word and by His deeds. As Jesus taught them, He tested them, sending them out to do as He did when they were ready. Even then, they continued being His disciples, being taught by the Holy Spirit.

According to Acts 11:19, the gospel was only preached to the Jews prior to this event in Antioch. It is interesting that before word could be sent via Barnabas that the Gentiles could also believe in Jesus, the gospel was already spreading to the Gentiles to great effect. It seems the Jewish believers were not referred to as Christians at that time.

According to Acts 11:26, the term *Christian* in the Bible applied to a disciple or follower of Jesus Christ. Note it does not refer to a member of a congregation, denomination, or sect. Following Christ does not involve belonging to a group. It involves personally following the teachings of Jesus Christ. It involves doing what Jesus did. It involves taking up your cross daily to follow Him in obedience to His command.

There is no prerequisite of belonging to a Christian denomination or organization. A Jew who follows Jesus is still a Jew and may congregate with other Jews and practice their traditions. Likewise, a Muslim can follow Jesus and still congregate with other Muslims and practice their traditions. What is required to follow Jesus is to believe in Him, to learn what He taught, and to do as He commanded.

Today, to be called a Christian only implies you go to a church that teaches salvation through Christ. In many cases, it simply means your family has been called Christian for generations. Church attendance is optional. Baptism is optional. Being Christian in this manner does not require you to have a relationship with Him, to know anything about Him, or to be actively seeking Him. The only requirement is that your father and/or mother were Christians, their grandparents were Christians, and their great grandparents were Christians, making you Christian by familial tradition. To these people, being a Christian means you celebrate Christmas to get presents in the winter and celebrate Easter to eat chocolate bunnies and hard-boiled eggs in the spring.

Biblically, to be a Christian literally means to *follow* Christ (see Luke 9:23-26). It means having a close intimate relationship with Jesus and wanting to be conformed to His image. You want to follow where He leads you, which is into the presence of God, our Heavenly Father. Most of those who call themselves Christian have never entered into the presence of God. In many cases, they have not actually had an encounter with Jesus.

To be a follower of Christ means to take up His burden for the lost, to lead them into the presence of the Living God, and to restore that broken relationship with their Heavenly Father. It means to put aside the preoccupations of this life and live as He would. Very few "Christians" want to leave this life of carnal pleasures behind for an abundant life in Him. Their faith is focused on what He can do for them instead of seeking to know what they can do for Him. Their prayers are to give me, heal me and prosper me. Their prayers are one-sided conversations with God; they never pause to hear God's response.

Jesus died for one purpose: to open the way for us to be restored to the Father. To be a Christian is to walk upon that way into the Father's presence and then to return to lead others to Him. Christ did not die to establish yet another religion, but to heal man's broken relationship and to restore each of us in fellowship with God. The word fellowship does not refer to a church potluck but to a partnership with Jesus, continuing His work here in the world.

Jesus wanted us to pursue a relationship with the Father. I do not use the word pursue lightly. Pursuing a deep relationship with God requires commitment, dedication, and communication. Just as in any relationship we may form here with friends, coworkers, or family, it takes time and communication to develop that relationship.

Jesus is the key to obtaining a restored relationship with God. Jesus gathered disciples to Himself to teach them and show them the way back to God. He taught by the Word and by His example. The disciples He called literally left their families, communities, and jobs to follow Him. They chose to wander through Judea without any baggage in order to follow Jesus. Think about that.

The disciples followed Him for years, learning twenty-four hours a day, living with Him, eating with Him, sleeping on the ground with Him. They watched and listened as He was questioned and tested by the religious leaders of the day. They shared in His reputation and in His persecution. They identified with Him in every way. They grew in knowledge and spiritual discernment until Jesus could send them forth to do as He did.

He began to teach them spiritual realities through parables. How do you teach the blind to see and the deaf to hear? You use what they are familiar with to describe what they are missing. The parables were teaching tools that used concepts the disciples were familiar with to teach them spiritual principles that could only be understood using their spiritual senses. He began teaching them about the kingdom of God and the kingdom of heaven using stories.

> "Then said Jesus to those Jews which believed on him, If ye continue in my word, then are ye my disciples indeed; And ye shall know the truth, and the truth shall make you free" **(John 8:31-32)**.

Discipleship as we know it today is really about teaching new believers the main doctrines of the denomination or church they have chosen to attend; such appears to be the entire purpose of this religious program. Largely, there are discipleship classes that meet maybe once a week for an hour to teach some basic doctrines. The discipleship classes last a few months, and then people can choose to progress to other Bible studies, prayer meetings, and services (or not).

Discipleship in the early church was different. The purpose was to bring the believer into an intimate relationship with God, starting with basic doctrines that could be understood with the natural mind. In the book of Hebrews, Paul referred to those basic doctrines as "milk". Paul then went on to say that they could not receive what he was saying about Christ being the High Priest because they were "dull of hearing."

Of whom we have many things to say, and hard to be uttered, seeing ye are dull of hearing. For when for the time ye ought to be teachers, ye have need that one teach you again which be the first principles of the oracles of God; and are become such as have need of milk, and not of strong meat. For every one that useth milk is unskilful in the word of righteousness: for he is a babe. But strong meat belongeth to them that are of full age, even those who by reason of use have their senses exercised to discern both good and evil. **Hebrews 5:11-14**

Paul stated they could not receive "strong meat" because their senses were not sufficiently developed to receive it. Paul was not talking about their natural senses nor their natural understanding but about their spiritual senses and understanding. As I meditated on this passage, the Spirit showed me they had trouble hearing or discerning the Spirit speaking to them. They relied only on their natural understanding and therefore created a set of doctrines, expecting those doctrines were enough to understand Christ and follow Him.

Paul, being a man, could only share "milk' with the church. It was only through the spirit of revelation that men could receive and understand "strong meat." Paul basically told those first believers that he needed to start their discipleship all over again, teaching them anew the milk of the basic doctrines in order to lead them into developing their spiritual senses.

That the God of our Lord Jesus Christ, the Father of glory, may give unto you the spirit of wisdom and

revelation in the knowledge of him: The eyes of your
understanding being enlightened; that ye may know
what is the hope of his calling, and what the riches of
the glory of his inheritance in the saints, And what
is the exceeding greatness of his power to us-ward
who believe, according to the working of his mighty
power. **Ephesians 1:17-19**

One of the purposes of the Holy Spirit is to impart a
personal revelation of Christ to the believer. The Spirit
makes plain the power that was in Christ is also in
the believer who has his understanding enlightened.
If the believer's spiritual senses are not developed,
all they can expect is a religious experience, not a
spiritual experience, because they cannot hear the
Spirit speaking to them.

What are those spiritual senses? Let us start with the
sense of spiritual hearing.

Jesus answered them, I told you, and ye believed not:
the works that I do in my Father's name, they bear
witness of me. But ye believe not, because ye are
not of my sheep, as I said unto you. My sheep hear
my voice, and I know them, and they follow me: And
I give unto them eternal life; and they shall never
perish, neither shall any man pluck them out of my
hand. **John 10:25-28**

Jesus said quite clearly in this passage that those
who follow Him hear His voice. He was not referring
to their natural hearing but their spiritual hearing.
Hearing is perhaps the most important of our spiritual
senses. Knowing God's voice is not dependent on
Jesus's sacrifice on the cross because the prophets

heard God speaking long before Jesus was born. Faith depends greatly on hearing God speak: "So then faith cometh by hearing, and hearing by the word of God" (Romans 10:17).

There are two Greek words that translate to "word". The most familiar is *logos* which refers to the written Word and applies to the entire Bible. The second is *rhema* which refers to "utterance." In this verse, it refers to the utterance of God or of God speaking directly to the believer. A person's faith is strong when the believer recognizes God is speaking directly to him. This verse from Romans speaks about how faith depends on spiritually hearing from God (Father, Son and Holy Spirit). Perhaps now we can understand why Jesus constantly asked His disciples why their faith was so small. The disciples were still learning to exercise their spiritual sense of hearing.

When we recognize God's voice speaking to us, we can start to walk in faith and see God move through us as we submit and obey His will.

> For these are not drunken, as ye suppose, seeing it is but the third hour of the day. But this is that which was spoken by the prophet Joel; And it shall come to pass in the last days, saith God, I will pour out of my Spirit upon all flesh: and your sons and your daughters shall prophesy, and your young men shall see visions, and your old men shall dream dreams: And on my servants and on my handmaidens I will pour out in those days of my Spirit; and they shall prophesy. **Acts 2:15-18**

There are other spiritual senses as well. Spiritual sight is expressed in visions and dreams that come from God. There is a very different character between natural dreams and spiritual dreams. Natural dreams tend to be chaotic and supposedly are the subconscious mind trying to deal with the experiences of the day. Spiritual dreams are clear, involve God and can usually be remembered afterwards. God can reveal His purpose for you, or other revelations, in a dream (asleep) or vision (awake).

Another spiritual sense is to know when the power of God is flowing in you or through you. Some confuse this as feeling the presence of God. God is always present in the believer and you cannot *feel* Him. However, you can spiritually feel His power moving in you. This happens either when He is performing a work in you or through you into the world.

You can feel this power moving through you when you share His thoughts with those around you or when you are obedient in doing what He calls you to do at a particular moment. This is how we know when we are operating in the gifts of the Spirit. When you impart a word *(rhema)* of God in a message from the pulpit, or during a Bible class or during a one-on-one testimony sharing the gospel, God allows you to feel His power flow through you, confirming that He is the source of the Word that was sent forth.

> "So shall my word be that goeth forth out of my mouth: it shall not return unto me void, but it shall accomplish that which I please, and it shall prosper in the thing whereto I sent it" **(Isaiah 55:11)**.

The Holy Spirit constantly works on our paradigm or viewpoint of reality. As a babe in Christ, we start with a viewpoint of reality aligned with the way the world taught us to see the natural world. This view excludes any sense of the reality of the spiritual nature we all have. As the Spirit of Revelation moves in us, our paradigm shifts toward understanding the world from God's viewpoint, integrating our spiritual nature into our identity.

To summarize, discipleship begins with the teaching of the basic doctrines (milk) by men who are spiritually mature. The purpose of this stage is to aid the beginning believer in developing their spiritual senses. Lack of the development of spiritual senses results in the reestablishment of religion as a substitute for knowing God. All of the epistles in the New Testament were letters sent to the first churches to encourage them not to settle for more religion but to go on to a true relationship with the Father. That is when the believer can be taught "strong meat" directly by the Holy Spirit. When the Holy Spirit takes over the lessons, the believer can truly be a disciple of Christ.

Recognizing God's Will

Our ability to know God's will for us requires us to develop our spiritual senses. Developing these spiritual senses takes time and dedication on our part. The primary sense we need is the spiritual sense of hearing. The other spiritual senses will come as you begin to hear His voice and submit to His will. In my walk, I have defined three keys that helped me recognize when God is speaking to me.

God created us capable of hearing His voice. He breathed His Spirit into Adam when He created him, so, through Adam, we have a spiritual nature (see Genesis 2:7). Over time, man's spiritual nature grew weak because men no longer spent time walking and talking with God. Only a few men sought God and strengthened their spiritual senses enough to hear Him; mainly the prophets of the Old Testament. One of Jesus's tasks was to teach His disciples about their spiritual nature. He breathed upon them to restore their ability to hear His voice in their spirits. He also gave the disciples the Holy Spirit prior to the Pentecostal event in the book of Acts.

Then said Jesus to them again, Peace be unto you: as my Father hath sent me, even so send I you. And when he had said this, he breathed on them, and saith unto them, Receive ye the Holy Ghost: Whosesoever sins ye remit, they are remitted unto them; and whose soever sins ye retain, they are retained. **John 20:21-23**

KNOWING GOD'S WORD

Everyone hears God, even those who do not know Jesus. The problem is, in the flesh, most people do not expect to hear His voice. If we have not trained our spiritual senses to recognize His voice, we will not be able to hear Him. First, we need to understand our thoughts are not all our own. Our mind is where our spirit and flesh meet. God's voice originates in our spirit and speaks to us in the thoughts passing through our mind. The voice of the enemy originates in our flesh and plants thoughts in our mind to lead you away from God. Our own thoughts are influenced by God and by the tempter, but we decide which thoughts to entertain and submit to. If we do not exercise our spiritual senses, the tempter's voice will be easier to hear since his voice appeals to our flesh.

Let me share an example from my life. When my wife and I go to town, we often see disabled and homeless people around the plaza asking for money. My first thought is one of mercy, and I start to reach for my wallet. Immediately, other thoughts counter the action, telling me I need the money to buy something I need or want, or that the government will help these people, or any other number of reasons why I should just keep walking. The first thought is of God. My God is a sacrificial God, and His voice often calls us to give up something to help others. The following thoughts are of the enemy trying to tempt me to ignore God's voice. I am the one who needs to decide what to do. How many times does God speak to me and I choose instead to follow the voice of the enemy simply because I cannot recognize what was happening? Now, I am aware of the enemy and his temptations and I am free to recognize and submit to God's voice instead.

In my experience, it is rare to hear God speak in a manner that seems as if His voice is literally audible. I have experienced this perhaps three or four times in my walk with Him. He may speak as I walk in this world and see a need. His voice always speaks through my mind while I meditate on His Word. Often as I meditate, the verse I am considering triggers other verses to come to mind. Through the Holy Spirit, I am able to connect them, clarify them, and amplify them in a way that reveals to me God's will, character, and purpose. I visualize these verses as a sprinkling of drops of His living water creating intersecting ripples on a smooth pond of the Spirit in my mind, each ripple a reflection of a related verse. It is really difficult to describe a spiritual experience in mundane words, but I am trying.

The most difficult and time-consuming part of knowing His voice is in reading, memorizing, and meditating on the Bible. This is where most Christians fall short in their walk with God. When you are just starting, you tend to read the Bible with an intellectual mindset and do not understand much. You may be following a program of reading the Bible in a year, and at the end of the year, you realize you really did not get much out of it. This is normal. The Bible is not a book you read once and put back in your bookcase. Rather, search through the Bible and let the Holy Spirit guide your study. You will find it becomes much more interesting as you go.

You may choose a Bible that is easy to read and those are usually a transliteration of the Bible. In other words, those versions put the meaning of the verses in a modern or easy-to-read context. There are limited study materials available for them. For serious study, I recommend a Bible that is a word-for-word translation of the original Hebrew and Greek texts, such as the King James Version I use. Other word-for-word translations are the New King James Version, the New American Standard Bible, the English Standard Version, and the Amplified Bible. There are Bible dictionaries and concordances for these Bible translations that will be useful in your studies. A parallel Bible, one which has several versions side by side, may also help.

Something else you need to understand is that not every passage in the Bible is God speaking. For instance, Job's friend Eliphaz tried telling him there must be some sin Job committed that brought this disaster upon him (see Job 4:7-8) when his tribulations were actually a test to prove Job's faithfulness. It would be a mistake to quote Eliphaz and attribute what he said to God. However, everything in the Bible is there because it is useful in teaching us, whether that be about the history of the Jewish nation, the development of Jewish religion, or about the times and teachings of Jesus. As James said, "All scripture is given by inspiration of God, and is profitable for doctrine, for reproof, for correction, for instruction in righteousness: That the man of God may be perfect, thoroughly furnished unto all good works" (James 3:16-17).

There are two Greek words that are translated as "word" in the New Testament. The Bible is the written Word *(logos)*, and Jesus is the written Word manifested (see John 1:1-14). *Rhema* is another Greek word that is translated as "word" in the Bible but which is defined in Strong's as "utterance." When used in conjunction with the phrase "of God," it refers to God speaking. An example is found in Romans 10:17: "So then faith cometh by hearing, and hearing by the word of God." This verse says that spiritual hearing comes when you recognize God is speaking directly to you. When you recognize He is speaking to you, faith in being able to do what He is asking of you becomes easy.

The first thing I do when I read the Bible is ask the Holy Spirit to guide me. As I read, there are times when a passage or verse will jump out at me. It is almost like that verse was printed in **bold letters**. This is how I experience a *rhema* word where God wishes to communicate something to me. I then commit this passage to memory, study it in context using dictionaries and concordances, and meditate on it, seeking revelation from the Holy Spirit throughout. I find this to be the best way to study the Bible.

So, the first key to knowing God is speaking to you is recognizing and verifying those thoughts passing through your mind are in complete harmony and agreement with His written Word and are His thoughts. For the believer to start on this journey requires him to know and understand the Word of God. As you receive revelation from the Spirit concerning the Word, God's voice becomes clearer and your understanding of the Word becomes deeper.

A warning though. The enemy tries to speak through the scriptures as well. An example of this was when Jesus was led by the Spirit into the wilderness to be tempted, as related in Matthew 4:6 and in Luke 4:10-11. Satan knows scripture and does his best to twist its meaning to tempt us. Jesus recognized Satan's manipulation of what was written and responded with direct quotes of God's Word. Jesus knew His Father's character and purpose and was not confused by the enemy.

KNOWING GOD'S CHARACTER

The second key to recognizing God's voice is important but cannot be known without the first key. The second key is to know God's character.

> "Let this mind be in you, which was also in Christ Jesus: Who, being in the form of God, thought it not robbery to be equal with God" **(Phil. 2:5-6)**.

These verses tell us we should be like God in the same way Jesus was. We need, therefore, to know God's character. Jesus is our example of God's character since He identified so closely with His Father. To see Jesus is to see the Father: "Jesus saith unto him, Have I been so long time with you, and yet hast thou not known me, Philip? he that hath seen me hath seen the Father; and how sayest thou then, Show us the Father?" (John 14:9).

As we examine Jesus's character, we can clearly see God's character. Jesus was holy, sacrificial, loving, slow to judge, quick to forgive, and just. God's voice will not tell you to do something that is counter to His character. For instance, He will not tell you to judge (meaning condemn) others but to forgive them. He will not tell you to act out of hate or fear, seeking vengeance or retribution. He will not tell you to divorce your spouse to marry someone else that He "chose" for you because He is holy. He will never speak out of character.

The enemy will send thoughts telling you to do all those things. Recognizing the enemy and his temptation is most of the battle. When you know who is speaking in your thoughts, you can pick whose thoughts to submit to. The choices you make between those thoughts determines who will guide you: God or the enemy.

KNOWING GOD'S PURPOSE

The third key to recognizing God's voice is to understand God's purpose. God does not do anything that does not align with His purpose.

> "For God so loved the world, that he gave his only begotten Son, that whosoever believeth in him should not perish, but have everlasting life" **(John 3:16)**.

Mankind is so egocentric and only thinks of the world in the terms of human civilization. But the word for "world" *(kosmos)* used in the verse above pertains to ALL of His creation. Mankind has a role in His creation—to serve as this world's caretakers. He gave Adam and Eve the responsibility to care for this world. That responsibility passed on to us. It was never taken back, even after the fall. All of God's creation is waiting for its caretakers to restore their relationship with God. Under God's direction, the damage mankind has wrought on this earth can be healed. "For the earnest expectation of the creation eagerly waits for the revealing of the sons of God" (Rom. 8:19).

We are called to do His will, not our own. Yet, as Jesus had to suffer to do His Father's will, why do we think we will not be called to sacrifice as well? "For it is God which worketh in you both to will and to do of his good pleasure" (Phil. 2:13). When God's voice asks you to sacrifice, whether it is from your finances, time, or other things you count as important, you need to respond as Jesus did in the Garden of Gethsemani: "... not My will, but Yours, be done" (Luke 22:42b).

Having made known unto us the mystery of his will, according to his good pleasure which he hath purposed in himself: That in the dispensation of the fulness of times he might gather together in one all things in Christ, both which are in heaven, and which are on earth; even in him: In whom also we have obtained an inheritance, being predestinated according to the purpose of him who worketh all things after the counsel of his own will: That we should be to the praise of his glory, who first trusted in Christ. **Ephesians 1:9-12**

God's plan has always been to restore His relationship with man, and not just with man in general, but with each and every one of us as individuals. The good news is that God wants a personal relationship better than the relationship He had with Adam and Eve. That relationship was between Creator and creature. Through Christ, we can enter a relationship with God reflecting one between the Father and His children.

So, God's purpose is to restore His creation by restoring His relationship with us. Any voice you hear that is not aligned with either restoring your relationship with Him as one of His children, connecting other lives to His (sharing the Good News), or caring for His creation in this world is not a voice you should pay attention to.

Knowing God's Word, God's character, and God's purpose can help you to recognize His voice when He speaks to you. Let His Spirit guide you into an ever-deepening relationship with Him where He reveals to you His will for you, not just in general, but in the specific role He has chosen you to assume. You can know God's will, but you must decide to seek Him out with diligence and dedication to enact it. Do you want to know His will for you?

Conclusion

Religion alone will never bring you into an intimate relationship with God. The Holy Spirit is given to us for that purpose. Settling for the doctrines of men will lead to a powerless Christian walk that may look appealing from the outside but will never be able to satisfy that inner yearning for more. The surface waters of religion are subject to the stormy winds of conflict and debate, but the deep waters are calm and satisfying.

The Holy Spirit wants to reveal the deep currents of the Spirit to those who diligently seek Him. This is the reward spoken of in Hebrews: "But without faith it is impossible to please him: for he that cometh to God must believe that he is, and that he is a rewarder of them that diligently seek him" (Heb. 11:6).

The Holy Spirit is the revealer of the deep things of God, but He cannot reveal those things to those who are deaf, dumb, and blind spiritually. He is the Spirit of Revelation and wants to move us into the deep waters of our spiritual nature. Only then can we truly experience what it is to be His body.

My purpose in writing this book is simple. I want to encourage you to move beyond a merely intellectual understanding of the Bible. I want to show you what Jesus achieved on the cross was meant for much more than establishing yet another religion. Please consider whether you are truly satisfied with your current religious experience or if you yearn for something deeper, more powerful, and more like the relationship Jesus had with the Father. I know the Father is waiting on your decision and truly desires a profound relationship with you. Seek the guidance of the Spirit. He will gladly lead you into the deep currents of the Spirit, where you can discover the reality of your spiritual nature and of our Father's endless love for you.

Made in the USA
Columbia, SC
27 August 2024

41247691R00078